Artificial Intelligence:
Unorthodox Lessons

How to Gain Insight and Build Innovative
Solutions

Pedram Ataee, Ph.D.

Notice of Copyright

First published in 2020
Copyright © Pedram Ataee 2024

Ataee, Pedram
Artificial Intelligence: Unorthodox Lessons: How to Gain Insight and Build Innovative Solutions

Imprint: Independently published

My journey into artificial intelligence began in 2005 when I became familiar with the beautiful concept of manifold learning. My attraction to this subject went hand-in-hand with my love of mathematics since topics such as linear algebra, analytic geometry, and probability theory are part of understanding and implementing manifold learning techniques. Using these methods, I was able to create a face recognition engine. Manifold learning techniques enabled me to interpret high-dimensional data that would otherwise be difficult to analyze. The skills inherent in those techniques allowed me to understand the fundamentals better and, moving forward, helped me to solve problems better. I felt empowered.

In 2013, I started learning natural language processing, or NLP, with the assistance of a compelling library named NLTK (the Natural Language Toolkit). That year, I had the opportunity to be part of an innovative company working on a gesture control armband. The company aimed to build an armband that could fit the forearm and recognize hand gestures based on muscle signals. At the time, I was in charge of developing an AI-based recognition engine that could run on a microcontroller and address a multitude of consumers. I invented what we termed a muscle language and an ensemble classifier, and together, they were used to design a gesture detection engine. The algorithm had to function on a low computational power processor and still work fine for our users. It was a successful project.

In 2015, my friend and I (a mechanical engineer and an AI engineer, respectively) took on the task of building a computer vision solution for the automotive industry. Precisely, we were asked to develop a particle detection solution. In doing so, we had to design and build our data collection setup, which required knowledge of other topics, including, but not limited to, fluid dynamics. We were able to figure out what we needed to do because certain members of our team were knowledgeable about the laws of fluid dynamics. We designed an imaging chamber that did not trap particles in it as we knew that a problematic imaging setup for data collection could create unresolvable problems down the road. It was while working on this project that I came to realize, deep in my heart, the truly significant nature of data quality.

In 2018, I joined a company that was seeking to build an NLP-based solution to interpret regulatory documents. In order to accomplish this interpretation, we developed parsing engines that could read the documents and then structure the subsequent data to be used in NLP models for further interpretation. To do this, knowing that NLTK had lost the game to spaCy for, in particular, industry solutions, we utilized the latter. Technology advances fast, and you (and I) must always be prepared to adapt as a result.

In the past 10+ years, I have held various responsibilities with several AI startups including serving as an engineer, team lead, consultant, and advisor. In this book, I attempt to convey the foremost lessons I have acquired over the years. Although these experiences may not be taught in classrooms or found in classic textbooks, I am delighted to share them with you here.

Artificial intelligence is an advanced technology that can be utilized to build innovative solutions. To shape such results, you must learn the fundamentals of AI taught in our schools. However, to drive innovation in the AI field and solve the challenges you will be presented with your work, you also need to gain additional insight into this discipline. You can think of the fundamentals as an engine and the additional insight as the oil that helps an engine work. To gain this critical understanding, I encourage you to use any available resources and whatever learning techniques suit you best. I sincerely hope that this book can help you reach your goals.

This book is written, above all, for artificial intelligence directors and engineers with some experience in the field. For instance, you may be an AI executive with no technical background or an AI engineer who has successfully implemented several projects. This book was written with you in mind. The practical tips and insight will make you more productive regarding development and more prosperous in communication with other professionals. Through sharing my experiences building AI products, I have strived to describe sophisticated concepts in simple words. I hope you enjoy reading this book.

Furthermore, if you have any comments or questions, you are welcome to email me at pedram@dancewithdata.com. I would be delighted to hear from you.

CONTENTS

PART 1: AI WILL TRANSFORM YOUR BUSINESS 9

A Solution to Modern World Dilemmas: Artificial Intelligence..................... 11

How to Evaluate the Viability of AI in Your Business 21

How to Structure Your AI Consulting Service 29

How to Create a Perfect AI Strategy...35

How to Safeguard Your AI Product Strategy 41

The Key to Success in Enterprise AI: Chain of Values 47

PART 2: DATA, DATA, DATA 51

How to Create a Perfect Data Strategy 53

Significant Issues Connected with Large-Scale Data Collection..................61

Feature Selection: Exhaustive vs. Cherry-Picked 69

Four Common Mistakes to Avoid When Building an ML Product................73

How to Improve Data Quality in RAG Systems.............................81

PART 3: BUILDING AN EFFECTIVE AI SOLUTION....................... 87

Deep Learning in Simple Words..89

The Achilles Heel of AI Methods: Similarity Metrics 103

Word2vec Models are Simple Yet Revolutionary 109

How to Improve Single LLM Performance with Multi-Agent Systems 119

The Black Swan of the AI Industry: Ensemble Classifiers............................125

The Key to Success: Experiment Management Systems 135

The Key to Success: Explainable AI 139

PART 4: LEARN MORE 145

The Best Online Artificial Intelligence Courses 147

Part 1: AI Will Transform Your Business

A Solution to Modern World Dilemmas: Artificial Intelligence

In 2020 (and beyond), the world suffered through the COVID-19 pandemic and its different issues and challenges. "Problems" such as COVID-19, which deliver so much uncertainty and ambiguity, require innovative solutions. Because of the pandemic, we as a society faced significant questions, including "Who is more vulnerable to the coronavirus?" and "How can we treat patients who have contracted the coronavirus?" AI cannot respond to every question that arises due to what I will refer to as modern world dilemmas, but if utilized correctly, it can answer some of them.

In this chapter, I describe how AI could solve a real-world problem within the context of COVID-19. Although I have chosen the coronavirus as my example, the methodology I describe can also be generalized to other pressing modern-world dilemmas. I then end this chapter with some commentary on several ethical challenges related to artificial intelligence that I passionately believe must be considered (and resolved) as we build an AI-powered world.

Artificial Intelligence Vs. Mathematical Models.

The immune system is the most crucial biological system for fighting viruses in the human body. For years, researchers have worked to design mathematical models to describe the immune system and how viruses interact.

The mathematical models were developed to discover more effective responses to viral diseases such as the human immunodeficiency virus (HIV). The prototypes helped to uncover many unknowns, but they had shortcomings. For example, when mathematical models were used to analyze a biological system, it was preferable to analyze the system in isolation, as the more complex the model became, the less effective it performed.

To properly study COVID-19, we must examine several biological systems simultaneously. In contrast to mathematical models, AI is well-suited for complex problems. I would submit that now (the summer of 2020) is the perfect time to switch our approach.

AI Is Well-Suited For Multifarious Problems With Many Unknowns.

Experts agree that individuals with underlying conditions are more vulnerable to the coronavirus. These conditions include, but are not limited to, heart diseases, hypertension, diabetes, and chronic respiratory disorders. Yet, we have learned that the coronavirus and its variants also affect young people with no known underlying maladies. This is but one of the many unknowns surrounding COVID-19, and we need to harness the power of technology to solve these mysteries.

Understanding the reasons for why some individuals are particularly vulnerable to the coronavirus is a multifarious problem. AI can definitely help answer some of the challenging issues surrounding the virus, but only if utilized properly.

More granularity on underlying conditions is needed to provide better healthcare to vulnerable individuals and better care for our communities' residents. For example, with more knowledge, medical professionals might decide that it is best to separate individuals into several groups using a multi-level risk schema rather than a standard two-level risk schema comprised of high—and low-risk levels.

Although AI can be used relatively easily to identify at-risk individuals, it is essential to note that not all identified underlying conditions have the same risk level. Finding a more personalized response is crucial since a considerable percentage of the world's population deals with at least one of these underlying conditions.

AI Will Disappoint You Without Diverse, Vast, And Relevant Data.

An AI solution requires a bulk of diverse and relevant data to extract useful information, even more so when little is known about the problem being examined. The AI solution will disappoint you if the correct amount and data type are not used.

What Does It Mean For Data To Be Diverse?

Using only one relevant data type to solve a problem with many unknowns is not recommended, as AI solutions can extract the significance of each data type. Thus, you should collect various relevant data regardless of its importance. If you doubt the usefulness of certain data, the best practice is to still collect the data and then let AI compute its relevance.

 An AI solution requires a bulk of diverse and relevant data in order to extract useful information, and even more so when little is known about the problem being examined.

For instance, regarding COVID-19, an individual's weight can be one factor, but if no other information is collected, a person's weight is probably not very useful information on its own. Whenever possible, diverse data is needed for each individual, such as weight, blood test results, medical history, etc. These data types, though, should be selected based on medical experts' opinions on what personal information is the most useful.

What Does It Mean For Data To Be Vast?

Solutions derived from AI require a large amount of data to be effective and appropriate. With that stated, more data does not always guarantee better results. Nevertheless, a practical AI solution cannot be built upon a small dataset. A rule of thumb is to have at least 10x more data points whenever a new data field is added to your dataset. You should always balance the number of data points in your dataset with the number of data fields. Chapter 10 describes common mistakes you should do your best to avoid when using AI.

As explained, a considerable volume of data is crucial to building AI solutions. However, the data must have a sufficient volume from each class of targets, which can also be referred to as having a balanced dataset. For example, when collecting data within the COVID-19 context, data from individuals with various underlying conditions and those with none of the identified underlying conditions must be collected in a relatively similar portion.

In other words, avoid collecting a vast amount of data from individuals at low risk of contracting COVID-19 and less data from those at high risk. Chapter 8 explains some significant issues that can arise when conducting large-scale data collection.

What Does It Mean For Data To Be Relevant?

It is not recommended to use, for instance, an individual's height to determine their risk level for the coronavirus. It is obviously not relevant. Relevancy is rooted in the cause-and-effect relationship between the data and the problem being investigated. The field experts are the ones who can best differentiate between relevant and irrelevant data. For example, according to doctors, blood test results are crucial in the context of COVID-19.

In short, if you are confident that a particular piece of data is irrelevant, neglect it; however, if you have any doubts, collect it and let the AI solution extract its relevancy.

 Relevancy is rooted in the cause-and-effect relationship between the data and the problem being investigated. The field experts are the ones who can best differentiate between relevant and irrelevant data.

Blood test results are relevant to any investigation into COVID-19 since they represent body mechanisms such as the immune, endocrine, and cardiorespiratory systems. These test results contain the blood cells' counts and shapes, including white and red cells, which we know play essential roles in vital biological mechanisms. AI algorithms must, therefore, be exposed to such relevant data; otherwise, they will undoubtedly underperform.

AI, COVID-19, And Individual Vulnerability.

In what follows, I want to describe how artificial intelligence could be used to identify an individual's risk level for the coronavirus.

First, we must collect a large volume of diverse and relevant data from affected individuals. Since not much is known about COVID-19, all measurements from pertinent blood test results and other relevant data should be utilized. For the sake of simplicity and without the loss of generality, I emphasize blood test results in this section. I also want to mention that this book was updated and revised in the spring of 2021, so my comments are current to that time frame.

Medical professionals must collaborate with AI experts to determine the relevant required blood tests. We could begin with basic tests such as a complete blood count (to measure red and white cells in part), a C-reactive protein test (to measure the body's response to inflammation), and a hematocrit test (to measure red blood cells). Each recorded measurement is called a feature in the AI context.

Individuals could then be represented with a vector containing all these features, called a feature vector in AI lingo. Medical experts could then label the severity of each individual's illness. Given the feature vectors and labels, the problem would be well-formulated and capable of being deciphered by AI techniques.

We could use classification techniques to target the work further (if you are not familiar with them, the goal of classification techniques is to determine smaller groups that individuals belong to). In this case, each group would represent a specific body response to the virus, translating directly to each group's risk or vulnerability level.

After training an AI model, an individual's vulnerability could be predicted by feeding their blood test results into the model. AI could, therefore, help identify those individuals who, if they were to contract the coronavirus, would likely experience severe symptoms and require hospitalization, those who would likely experience only mild symptoms, and those who would likely not suffer any symptoms. As needed, more granularity could then (relatively) easily be incorporated into the modeling process.

If we can find a way to protect the privacy of data when making use of AI, AI solutions to many of the challenges that we face will very likely be just around the proverbial corner.

It is possible to use AI to identify an individual's risk level to the coronavirus; however, other challenges prevent us from obtaining such results. For example, to overcome the inherent execution challenges, we would require effective teamwork among medical professionals, AI experts, and governments.

I know that AI can solve many problems we face, but at the same time, we must ensure that AI solutions are developed responsibly. One of the substantial complications of using AI in healthcare is data privacy. For example, many AI experts are hesitant to work with sensitive data such as blood test results; however, finding solutions for privacy concerns is a much better option than simply not utilizing artificial intelligence. However, ethical challenges surrounding the development of AI solutions are not just limited to data privacy. I explain three more challenges in the next section.

AI Ethical Challenges.

Before reading this section, I ask you to drop your guard. I have studied and worked in AI for the past 15 years. I have an immense appreciation for the power of artificial intelligence. Therefore, for what follows, I intend not to devalue AI but to advocate for building AI solutions more responsibly.

Economic Inequality.

If you care about economic inequality, you should be cautious about using huge AI models such as GPT-3 (comprised of 175 billion parameters). When a model has that many parameters, you need a very high computation power to benefit from it. These models cannot be tuned with small datasets. Accordingly, extensive data collection is required to ensure this model is used to its total capacity. The question then is, how many AI experts have access to the necessary computation power at a reasonable cost to compete with the giant companies out there? In addition, how many small businesses have enough capital to conduct such a large-scale data collection at an affordable price? The answer is almost none.

This is, indeed, a never-ending game, and models will continue to become larger and larger. Consequently, only the giant companies will have the computation power to run these models, and small startups will have no chance to compete. This is not the future that I envision for artificial intelligence. We should not let the giant companies control the destiny of artificial intelligence.

I remember when creativity was the main growth engine in AI development. The more creative the algorithm was, the more powerful the model. I still believe creativity can, to some degree, beat the competition from the "super-large" models. It is (and will be) a tough challenge, but I can promise it will be a more exciting journey. I proved it myself while analyzing BERT and word2vec models; however, I am unsure what will ensue over the next ten years. What I do know for certain is that this is not how the AI story will end.

Global Warming.

Huge AI models have a substantial carbon footprint. For instance, some research shows autonomous vehicles require about 2500 watts per second to run on our streets. If this technology were to be deployed in every car in the world, it would impact global warming. If you care about the climate crisis, you should not use huge AI models irresponsibly. Please, stay on the right side of history.

We in the artificial intelligence community need to unite and push forward together with the ethical development of AI. We all desire a better future, and I know that artificial intelligence can help us to get there faster, but it cannot be allowed to damage our future in the process.

Prejudices And Biases.

Last but not least, we should fight against the biases in data. Since AI models might inherently adopt these biases, we must determine how to limit their effects. We know how badly current face recognition algorithms work for certain ethnic groups. We know how badly current speech recognition algorithms work for people with distinct accents. For all sorts of irrational and unacceptable reasons, our everyday interactions are full of prejudice and biases. We need to do what is necessary to prevent AI models from inheriting these biases from data.

The Last Words.

AI can drive innovative solutions for our most challenging difficulties if, and only if, we can formulate the problem well and collect the appropriate data. Until now, AI has changed our day-to-day lives with automated search or recommender systems, but we need AI to target more critical demands. If we can develop a personalized movie recommender, we must also advance personalized medical solutions.

For example, we need to be able to collect diverse and relevant data, such as blood test results. However, data privacy legislation usually treats blood test results as sensitive and protected information. Nonetheless, if we want to discover solutions for serious complications, we must incorporate such data. As members of the artificial intelligence community, one of our tasks must be to build an AI-powered world where ethics and privacy are paramount pillars.

CHAPTER 2

How to Evaluate the Viability of AI in Your Business

There is a misconception that artificial intelligence, or AI, can be used in every context. Even when it might seem appropriate at first glance, you, unfortunately, should not expect AI to solve every problem your business faces. When using AI in industry, you must always take a cautious approach since industry has many elements and variables that do not exist in academia, where AI is put to much use.

Numerous industry considerations, such as resource limitation and customer satisfaction, do not exist in academia. These considerations define both the technology development process and the formulation of the required acceptance criteria. In this chapter, I want to introduce an analytical framework that you can utilize to determine whether AI will suit your business needs.

AI In Simple Words.

With some exceptions, AI is a technology to design computer-assisted tools that will enhance the quality of decisions being made and/or escalate the number of decisions being reviewed. Below, I offer practical examples of how AI can benefit specific problems and situations.

Increase The Number Of Decisions Being Reviewed.

Humans cannot manually sift through, explore, and refine large volumes of data. For example, it is impossible to efficiently examine and process a large text, image, or voice dataset without using an AI-based analyzing engine.

Think of a business owner who wants to ensure compliance with a lengthy list of rules and regulations. It is expensive to hire an attorney to review all of the documents from various levels of government and extract all of the requirements they must abide by. With much less effort, an AI-based analyzing engine can translate complex documents into succinct compliance requirements that the company's employees can follow.

Improve The Quality Of Decisions Being Made.

When quality decisions are required, you will likely need access to expert advice. This can be due to several reasons, including a lack of financial or human resources. For example, medical specialists may be inaccessible wherever and whenever needed.

Think of a community that believes enhancing healthcare services for its residents is vital. There will be people in every community who suffer at least occasionally from, for example, skin diseases. However, the more rural the community, the closest skin care centers could be hundreds of miles (or kilometers) away. Building a medical center and hiring specialized staff for every ailment in every location is too costly. AI-based point-of-care (POC) devices can assist in deciding how truly urgent it is to pursue treatment for a specific skin condition. AI-based POC solutions can thus help remote locations receive certain healthcare services for almost every disease and ailment.

With some exceptions, AI is a technology to design computer-assisted tools that will enhance the quality of decisions being made and/or escalate the number of decisions being reviewed.

What Are The Common Applications Of AI?

In general, AI can perform tasks such as prediction, identification, perception, and optimization. Below are examples of these tasks.

- Predict weather conditions and events in the future using historical weather data or predict anticipated customer behavior using the behavior of previous customers.
- Identify underlying patterns to assist with fraud detection or to build predictive maintenance solutions using classification or clustering techniques.
- Perceive and analyze complex unstructured data to, for example, discover the abstract topics contained therein or to summarize large texts for quicker consumption.
- Optimize processes to enhance performance, such as when targeting personalized online advertisements or taking a precision medicine approach to treatment.

In all the above examples, representing a wide range of contexts, AI is used to improve the quality or quantity of decisions made through various data-driven methods. While these are typical applications, you cannot generalize them to every use case.

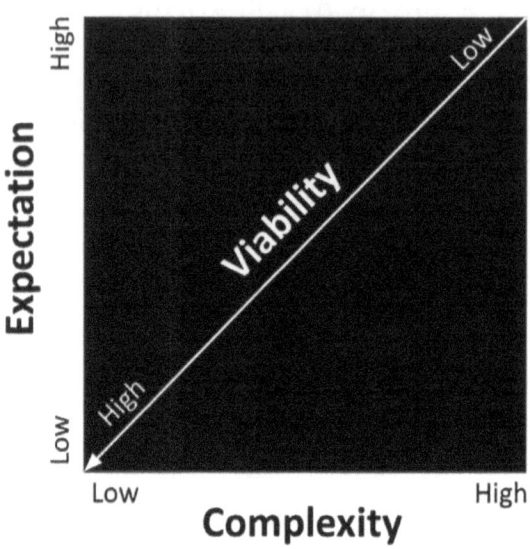

Figure 1- An analytical framework to evaluate the viability of using AI.

Expectation Vs. Complexity.

Suppose you want to use AI to solve a real-world business challenge. In that case, I strongly suggest using the "Expectation vs. Complexity" analytical framework, as illustrated in Figure 1 above. Should this framework not suggest viability in the use case, think twice before investing much time and/or money in the project. For example, if the complexity of a problem is high, and you are expecting a high performance from the AI engine, you need to be very cautious going forward.

Expectation.

"Expectation" refers to how beneficial you anticipate an AI-based solution will be for your business. It can be measured by a function built on three variables: quality, quantity, and value.

$$Expectation = f (quality, quantity, value)$$

- Quality refers to the expected performance associated with the use case. You may expect an analytical report or a Yes-No result from an AI solution (although its performance may not be as good as when used to create an analytical report). There are many standard metrics to measure performance, and you must design a metric suitable for the product in question, bearing in mind that you will always have to factor in metrics such as the false positive and false negative.
- Quantity refers to the number of times the AI-based solution is used in decision-making. For example, a small family may utilize an AI-based POC solution for skin care several times a year. However, an AI-based speech recognition solution that is included as a feature of a Smart TV will be used more than one thousand times a year in the same family.
- Value refers to the monetary value you earn or lose from each output generated by the AI-based solution. However, the value itself is rooted in the specific business use case. For example, failure prevention in the mining industry can create tremendous value even though failure may be rare. Thus, an AI solution with imperfect performance is still valuable to this industry.

The explicit definition of the Expectation function varies in each use case. Since neither the Expectation nor the Complexity function that follows is a complicated algebraic function, I thought it best to use this format to help you better understand the analytical framework I recommend.

You may expect to receive from an AI solution either an analytical report or a Yes-No result. If the business use case requires the latter, I encourage you to conduct additional analysis in order to confirm the viability of using AI in your business use case.

Complexity.

"Complexity" refers to how difficult it is to build an AI-based solution to solve a problem. It can be measured by a function based on three variables: data, technology, and problem.

$$Complexity = f\ (data, technology, problem)$$

Always allocate a considerable part of both your time and budget to collect clean, diverse, vast, and relevant data.

- Data- To solve a problem with AI, you must access a large volume of clean data, labeled or unlabeled. A large volume of clean data, particularly labeled data, is expensive, but it is virtually impossible to solve your problem without it. In short, AI will disappoint you without diverse, vast, and relevant data.
- Technology- Many problems that were not solvable five years ago may very likely be resolved today due to the fast advancement of technology. For example, computer vision did not find its place in the industry before the deep learning era. Nowadays, to solve many industry complications, many specialized deep neural network architectures with pre-trained

weights can be employed out of the box. Nevertheless, we still struggle to solve many problems due to technology challenges.

- Problem- Sometimes, problems are simply not solvable by AI. For instance, the long-term future value of a company's stock does not depend much on its historical values. Thus, AI cannot be used to predict future value. If AI were to be utilized, the results might not make sense regardless of model complexity. AI is used in algorithmic trading strictly for short-term predictions.

The explicit definition of the Complexity function differs in each use case. It is indeed demanding to measure complexity for a specific use case. That said, your use case can be benchmarked against existing cases in order to provide an estimate. If the intricacy of developing an AI-based solution is high, you may need to revise your development plan.

 Should the "Expectation vs. Complexity" analytical framework not suggest viability in the business use case, do think twice about making use of AI for the project.

The Last Words.

To build an AI solution, you will confront many challenges that consume time and money. At an early stage, I recommend you analyze your business case within the "Expectation vs. Complexity" analytical framework. If this framework suggests viability, you can then, with some measure of confidence, begin allocating your time and budget. If this framework does not suggest viability, you would be wise to explore other methods. I hope you will find value in using this analytical framework as part of your decision-making process.

CHAPTER 3

How to Structure Your AI Consulting Service

I n recent years, I have offered AI consulting services to several different companies. Most of them suffered from a lack of AI knowledge. Incompetency, and I sincerely use that word in a non-judgmental way, may create opportunities for experts to provide AI consulting services; however, it also creates many challenges when it comes to defining project requirements and deliverables. I personally have suffered through most of these trials. Whether you want to offer AI consulting services or, alternatively, if you require such services, please read this chapter carefully. I know it will be of benefit to you.

Business Understanding- Step 0.

In this initial step, you must determine the project's objectives and requirements. You must identify what the customer wants to accomplish and how the customer wants to measure its success. You need to define the required resources and the specific project requirements. In short, you should aim to answer the question: What does the business need?

After defining the business's objectives, you can determine the technical goals, i.e., what success looks like from a technical perspective. In this step, a technical requirement plan describing the required technologies and tools must be created.

Then, you should conduct a cost-benefit analysis. I designed the "Expectation vs. Complexity" analytical framework to perform the cost-benefit analysis in AI projects. You can learn more about this framework in Chapter 2.

Data Understanding- Step 1.

In this step, you must identify the data fields needed to train ML models. Then, you should write a plan explaining how you will collect the initial data set. The initial data is required for exploration and analysis purposes. Many unknowns concerning the data, such as quality and sufficiency, will be clarified during this process. In short, your aim is to answer the questions: What data do I have/need? Is it clean? Is it enough?

You then need to create a plan for large-scale data collection. Remember to document all of the quality issues and surface properties of the data in this step, including, for example, the relationships among the data and any insights you have gained through the process. I have found that visualization always helps me to dig deeper into the data and gain more insight. Basically, you want to do as much of the groundwork as you can at this early stage to have a well-thought-out plan to accomplish the customer's goals. You can read more about some of the significant issues arising when conducting large-scale data collection in Chapter 8.

Tip

In the early stages of a project, you must: (a) identify the data that will be required, (b) create a data collection plan, and (c) give serious consideration to how best you can go about analyzing the data that will be collected.

Data Preparation- Step 2.

In this step, you must decide on the data required for the large-scale data collection. Remember to always monitor and record the data quality during the data collection. Large-scale data collection is expensive, so it is important to plan ahead and decide how best to conduct it. In short, you should aim to answer the question: How can I best collect and organize the data?

The final dataset must be cleaned before proceeding to the next step. A common practice to clean or cure data is to correct, impute, or remove erroneous values. This is often the lengthiest step in the process. Without proper data curation, the project will encounter what I previously described as a "garbage in, garbage out" scenario.

The AI team may need to drive new attributes or features from the raw data while constructing the feature set. According to model architecture, you may also need to combine and reformat the existing data. For example, in many applications, string values are converted to numeric values, which helps you utilize mathematical operations on textual data. A famous example of data reformatting is the word2vec model, which is often used in text processing. You can read more about word2vec models in Chapter 14.

 Without proper data curation, your project will encounter what is called a "garbage in, garbage out" scenario.

Model Training- Step 3.

In this step, your job is to train and assess various machine learning (ML) models with different algorithms (e.g., Random Forest, XGBoost, or deep learning). This helps determine the best modeling techniques for the problem. Remember that the selected models will still require further tuning and evaluation. In short, you should aim to answer the question: What modeling techniques should be used?

No model can solve all problems. An ML model that fits problems with tabular data may not work for those with image data (and vice versa). In addition, an ML model that fits problems with small datasets may not work for problems with large datasets. And, of course, there are many more examples I could list!

Many people suppose model training or building is the most critical part of an AI project. This is not true, at least anymore. Using a large set of tools and libraries, such as the scikit-learn library, the model building itself can be summarized into a few lines of code. The AI team must compare multiple models against each other and interpret the results based on domain knowledge and performance metrics. You will also sometimes need to combine a series of models, a.k.a. an ensemble model, to gain performance. You can read about the story of an ensemble classifier that beats its competition in Chapter 16.

Many people suppose model training or building is the most important part of an AI project. This is not true, at least anymore.

Model Evaluation- Step 4.

In this step, you must extensively build, evaluate, and tune models to identify a model that meets the business requirements. Step 3 includes a series of evaluation tasks, focusing primarily on standard performance metrics. Most industrial problems require problem-specific metrics, and standard performance metrics are insufficient. In short, you should aim to answer the question: Which model best meets the business objectives?

Many industry problems are constrained by business and technical requirements other than machine learning criteria. For example, suppose you have a project that needs responses in literally less than one second. In that case, you must ensure it utilizes either low-computation techniques or machines with high computation power. As a second example, assume that you must process millions of images daily to improve your ML model by 1%. Is it really worth the effort?

You need to constantly review the work being accomplished using an experiment management system that helps to summarize results and identify any mistakes that are being made.

There is a significant difference between an AI model and an AI product. You must train many models with different parameter configurations to build an AI product. These models are trained using a training dataset that evolves over time. The performance metrics can also be changed according to various business requirements. Nevertheless, you must manage this complex process and identify the best model that meets the business objectives for multiple scenarios. To manage the evaluation process, you should use an experiment management system, which you will recall I wrote about in Chapter 17.

Model Deployment- Step 5.

In this step, you must create a thorough deployment, monitoring, and maintenance plan. The best model must be deployed on the cloud or on-premises to give your customers access. Most companies and experts look down on this step; however, a failure here may fail the whole project. In short, you should aim to answer the question: How do stakeholders access the results?

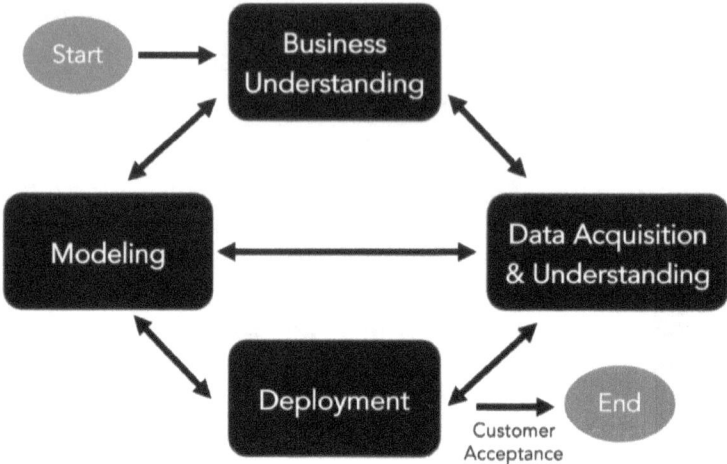

Figure 2- AI workflow.

A model is only applicable if the customer can access its results, it is updated to address unpredicted issues, and it complies with the customer's technical and business requirements. Figure 2 above is a visual representation of the AI workflow. You will note that customer acceptance is the final critical step. It would be best if you also remembered that cloud computing services can become costly, and this is especially true for computationally intensive ML models.

In the end, you must also take the time to review the entire process by conducting a project retrospective. Ensure that as part of the review, you answer these questions: (1) what went well, (2) what could have been better, and (3) what might be improved in the future. Lastly, to succeed in building AI products, you need to study the mistakes made by others. In Chapter 10, you can read about four more common mistakes that can arise when building an ML product and how to avoid them in your work.

CHAPTER 4

How to Create a Perfect AI Strategy

M ost new technologies start with considerable industry hype and slowly disappear from public view since they cannot meet our expectations for solving real-world problems. Artificial intelligence is one recent technology that has met and beaten its expectations. However, suppose you do not have a solid strategy when pursuing the development of an AI solution. In that case, your organization may abandon AI development due to an early failure to generate business value. You will likely do so before its potential has been adequately explored.

A Battlefield That Even Big Firms Struggle With.

I was talking with a friend who is a veteran trader in the stock market. He had been analyzing the Big Ideas 2021 deck the ARK Invest team created. In this report, they discussed their thoughts on emerging technologies and the future opportunities they present. My friend asked me to review the Deep Learning section and share my opinion. After reading through the deck, I certainly admired the quality of the content. However, I found parts that were not aligned with my experiences with AI and parts that I found insightful. Here, I want to provide some commentary about ARK's research and findings regarding deep learning.

- According to ARK, the required computation power for deep learning models will boost the AI chip industry. In recent years, deep learning models have become larger and larger, targeting the more complex and challenging problems that are being sought for solutions. Unfortunately, this does come with a cost. For example, the cost of model training in GPT-3 can reach millions of dollars. To train more powerful models, the computing resources devoted to model training have soared 10x each year in the past ten years. Many companies are also designing new chips tailored explicitly for deep learning models, either for inference or training purposes. At the same time, the AI industry has gradually embraced edge computing to ensure computation and storage occur at the point of use to improve data privacy and bandwidth efficiency. You can imagine a future where every consumer product has an AI chip inside, from your coffee machine and refrigerator to your autonomous vehicle. This future is now within our grasp, resulting in an incredible opportunity for the chip industry to develop and build a wide range of AI chips to address all of the various needs in the marketplace. I agreed[1].

- ARK believes the AI industry is rapidly advancing from computer vision to natural language processing. About the former, most mainstream applications such as object detection, semantic segmentation, pose estimation, and face recognition have been deeply investigated. You can now find off-the-shelf products or libraries that provide these services at a relatively reasonable price. However, we still struggle to design cost-effective, scalable, contextualized deep learning models in the context of NLP. The recent advancements seem promising. It consequently was not a stretch for professionals involved in this discipline to be able to predict that the focus of the AI industry is switching to natural language processing. I agreed.

---

[1] The ARK team has foreseen the recent advancement in the GPU industry that we observe today in 2024.

- In their Big Ideas 2021 deck, ARK references the OpenAI's GPT-3 "understands" language. This is a bold statement. Sometimes, we exaggerate in our business to push the technology and a project forward; however, this assertion goes beyond anything I can accept, even from the business perspective. As an AI expert, I know the challenges in this field. I am confident that GPT-3 solves some of them and helps to demonstrate that there is a light at the end of the tunnel. Nevertheless, we are still far from understanding language as a whole. I disagreed[2].

- ARK's "most provocative research conclusions" regarding deep learning claim that this technology can create more economic value than the internet did/does. Their comparison between deep learning and the internet is not completely correct, and I will explain my rationale below. Software as a service (or SaaS), the industry that represents the future of the internet, works beautifully in scale. This is not the case for deep learning. When the business logic of "how to scale" is developed in a SaaS product from the product perspective, the only challenge to scaling is setting up the cloud services accordingly. Since cloud services have progressed in recent years, in 2021, there is no tough hurdle for a SaaS product to scale. That is, the scaling issue is a two-sided problem in SaaS products, contrary to deep learning, which has many sides. For example, deep learning models are fragile to new data sets. The computation and efforts needed for fine-tuning, the process of capturing the essence of new data or use cases, are not negligible. The past performances of the models built do not necessarily hold when

---

[2] In 2024, after the introduction of GPT4o or Llama 3.1 with 405B parameters, we still struggle with understanding and responding to complex questions. Fact-checking and hallucinations are two significant challenges with LLMs.

you work toward edge cases, new use cases, or new data. Despite ARK's claims, there remain major challenges in deep learning, with reliability and maintainability being at or near the top of the list. In short, in my opinion, deep learning and SaaS are fundamentally different and cannot be compared. So, I disagreed.

The Three Main Pillars.

An AI strategy has three main pillars: Feasibility, Performance, and Scalability. Nowadays, everyone talks about the potential of AI models. Still, in what follows, I want to pinpoint the issues that must be investigated carefully to create the perfect AI strategy. A solid AI strategy will increase the chance of success in building your AI products.

Feasibility.

To build and launch an AI product, you will encounter many challenges. If you assume anything and everything is feasible in AI, you will almost certainly experience a sense of disillusionment. Many companies commence developing an AI product and then, in the middle of their project, figure out that what is underway will not work for them. That leads to disappointment and, more importantly, prevents them from correctly creating additional value for their business using AI. Before beginning to implement an AI solution, it is highly recommended that you (a) brainstorm with AI experts and (b) establish short-term and long-term goals for your AI mission.

For example, in some applications, the AI models must be implemented at the device level (a.k.a. Edge AI) to comply with data privacy legislation. Privacy concerns are minimized when the AI model is executed at the closest points to the data collection. However, applying AI models at this level creates many issues. For instance, you do not have access to powerful AI chips at this level compared to those you develop your cloud solution. Also, you cannot easily implement what you develop in a high-level programming language such as Python on programming languages compatible with Edge AI (e.g., C programming language) since the required libraries do not exist or are not easily transferable. As another example, let's assume you have started developing a deep-learning model for an application. Once begun, you realize that the necessary computation power and deep learning experts are either not accessible to you or, if they are, it is not cost-effective at all to utilize them. You may have to return to the proverbial drawing board if that situation unfolds.

Performance.

Every AI student has probably thought at least once, "Since so many standard metrics exist in the literature to help me evaluate the quality of a model, the performance of my AI model must be easy to measure." Unfortunately, that is not an entirely true conclusion. One major issue is that you can only measure your model's performance within the data you have collected. In other words, you must invariably deal with out-of-sample errors (a.k.a. generalization errors). No one can guarantee your user data. You can do your best to evaluate the AI model using a highly similar dataset to real-world data. Still, you will almost always be surprised by new and unexpected scenarios.

More importantly, most of the time (virtually without fail), you cannot guarantee the worst performance in an AI model. Many methods exist to reduce the generalization error; nonetheless, they are less successful at putting boundaries around mistakes, especially in gray-box models such as deep learning models. Moreover, a small perturbation in input data may introduce instability in the outcome, which is unacceptable in many use cases. You can read more about how to manage the performance of an AI model in Chapter 17.

Scalability.

It is easy to build AI models for a pilot project. However, it becomes more challenging when you develop an AI product and even harder when you decide to scale it. The Pareto Principle (a.k.a. the 80–20 rule) is valid here. Generally speaking, you can build an AI model that meets 80% of your expectations with 20% effort. You will be shocked at how hard it is to realize the remaining 20% of your expectations, especially when you want to scale the product in question.

The scalability challenges are rooted in, for instance, collecting a vast amount of clean and labeled data and then building a generalized model that can address most use cases. Both data collection and training in scale are expensive and intricate processes. The quality of an AI model is as good as its training data quality. You thus must ensure that the dataset used to train the AI model is comprehensive and will cover most use cases. In reality, the training dataset is not universally complete. That is why you will always encounter a bias-variance tradeoff when building an AI model. This tradeoff forces you to, for example, reduce the accuracy in your current dataset with the hope of increasing the accuracy in the dataset you have not yet collected.

Last, you must often build contextualized or finetuned models to address specific circumstances. Having one model that addresses several use cases is not often possible. AI models must be designed specifically for each industry or use case in which they are utilized. Even GPT4o or Llama 3.1 with 405B parameters still benefits from fine-tuning.

CHAPTER 5

How to Safeguard Your AI Product Strategy

I n AI startups, ensuring a solid product strategy requires careful consideration. This chapter highlights three important best practices: (a) determine the right use case, (b) don't oversell performance, and (c) build an automated pipeline. These practices are mainly the battlefield between sales and product teams. Aligning product and sales teams, focusing on realistic and value-driven tactics, will ensure success in AI ventures.

Feasibility — Determine The Right Use Case

Finding the proper use case that creates value for customers is the key. No one purchases a new product or solution unless they see the value. At the Enterprise level, the value mostly translates into "cost reduction." And if you can't deliver your solution in a way that reduces costs for your prospects, you can't gain their trust and, therefore, business.

First and foremost, you must be aware that AI is not suitable for every problem or situation. The problem may be ill-defined, the customer may not have the relevant data, or the technology may not be ready to address it. For example, LLMs are excellent at answering questions or summarizing texts. These tasks were challenging ten years ago but have become commodities today. In other words, ten years ago, technology was not ready to address summarization well enough, but many off-the-shelf solutions are available today.

> The problem may be ill-defined, the customer may not have the relevant data, or the technology may not be ready to address it. So, AI is not suitable for everything!

Determining the proper use case is difficult, but blindly pursuing use cases will cost you even more. The Expectation-Complexity framework will help you determine cases where AI can be used. If you are uncomfortable analyzing case by case, you can choose the well-known use cases in the industry. So, please don't choose the use case randomly. If you dream about use cases in your mind and think this or that use case is cool, you are making a big mistake! You can read more about The Expectation-Complexity framework in Chapter 2.

Performance — Don't Oversell And Confuse

Model performance is critical for data scientists and customers. However, you should avoid confusing customers by involving them in analyzing standard model metrics or setting unjust expectations (e.g., accuracy greater than 0.95). Let's say you are building a sales forecasting solution for a customer and want to compare two models. Which metric is better, RMSE or R2? What are the acceptable thresholds for these metrics? In the ideal world, we would like a scenario where RMSE=0 and R2=1. But that is not feasible.

You should not confuse your customers with data science metrics, including RMSE or R2. Data scientists use these metrics to build the best model. Customers must deploy the model in production and use their metrics to validate its quality. Allow the data science team to analyze models using these metrics and have customers evaluate them with their metrics.

Ensure the performance metrics are within reasonable ranges (e.g., R2 > 0.7). Using best practices, build a solid automated testing pipeline to improve model performance. The worst thing (believe me, the worst thing) is artificially inflating these numbers through malpractice, as this ruins everything. There is no magic! You just need to follow the best practices.

As a non-technical person, you may not be aware of the malpractices that inflate the model metrics. So, trust the opinions of an AI expert. Here are some examples of malpractices that can inflate model metrics:

- **Model Overfitting** — Training the model for too many epochs or features without proper validation.
- **Data leakage** — Including future or test data in the training set or using a feature with the information the model is trying to predict.
- **Improper cross-validation** — Using a simple train-test split without proper segmentation fails to eliminate biases.
- **Cherry-picking metrics** — Focusing only on metrics that show the model in a good light while ignoring others.
- **Hyperparameter tuning on test data** — Optimizing model parameters using the test set rather than a separate validation set.

Junior data scientists may unwillingly inflate model metrics by using the wrong practices. Choose your AI experts wisely.

Scalability — Build An Automated Data Pipeline

To build a high-performing model, you must create an automated pipeline to ingest and prepare data, train a model, and generate a performance report with one click. An automated pipeline is a requirement for building a scalable solution. Here is why this is important.

During AI development, improving model performance involves analyzing metrics over time. You are unlikely to achieve the best results in your first experiment. Therefore, you must set up the pipeline and run many experiments to reach your goal. The data pipeline must be consistent for all of these runs. Even a tiny difference in the data pipeline (or other parts of the pipeline) can invalidate your analysis! The only way to ensure the pipeline is identical across different trials is to build an automated pipeline with a one-click run command.

Tip

The only way to ensure the pipeline is identical across different trials is to build an automated pipeline with a one-click run command.

So, you should think twice if, for example, any of the following scenarios applies to you: (a) receive data from your customer through an email, (b) clean data out of the original pipeline, or (c) update the pipeline configs in every run.

The Last Words.

If you want to run a successful AI company, don't let anyone overlook the above points. Neglecting them will undoubtedly cause problems down the road.

These points impact your product strategy, and you should not allow anyone, especially the sales team, to change it. Every company has an ongoing battle between the product and sales teams. The sales team pursues its goal of meeting the sales quota by promoting random use cases, overlooking automated data pipelines, or overselling model metrics. You must guard your product and company from these mistakes.

 Build a successful product strategy through close collaboration between the sales and product teams. These teams must function in seamless integration, like a finely tuned system.

Everyone agrees that sales revenue is a company's growth engine. However, this doesn't mean you should rely purely on the sales team's decision to alter the product strategy, especially if they are not experienced with AI. Salespeople usually don't know much about AI and, therefore, need help understanding the impact of their decisions, which could significantly impact your company's success.

CHAPTER 6

The Key to Success in Enterprise AI: Chain of Values

In this chapter, I want to share the most important business lessons that I learned working with enterprise clients as an AI solution architect. These lessons may help some of you become more successful in delivering solutions to enterprise clients and securing business with them, especially if you are still in the negotiation process to sign a contract.

AI solution architects face many challenges when helping enterprises adopt AI. Enterprises may lack clean and structured data to start with or may not even be familiar with AI's potential. Many of these challenges are widely known, and you may already be prepared for them. However, there is one common challenging demand across every enterprise that can open all the doors if you properly address it: an end-to-end business solution with actionable and prescriptive insights. Here, I share lessons that I learned in this path through my experience working with a finance enterprise.

Finding a single use case for a finance enterprise is not hard, but the challenge is how to create an end-to-end business solution. Here, an end-to-end business solution refers to a sequence of use cases that sit back to back and solve a real problem. Each use case must come along with actionable and prescriptive insights to generate business value; otherwise, raw final results would not be that effective for the enterprise client. Before I forget, please don't confuse "end-to-end business solution" with the "end-to-end AI solution," which means a complete solution from the data prep step to the model deployment step. The business values generated in the sequence of use cases, along with actionable and prescriptive insights, is what I refer to as a "chain of values"!

— Single Use Case: Business Value with Actionable Insight

The first and foremost challenge in the AI enterprise world is to determine how to create business value. Your potential clients will not purchase your product or service if you can not show how they can gain from AI. The finance enterprise that I was working with was interested in the charge-off prediction use case as the main problem. When a creditor writes off a debt as a loss and decides not to go after collecting this debt, it is a charge-off case. They wanted a solution to predict the likelihood of customers' charge-offs.

The business value of a charge-off prediction solution was clear to the finance enterprise, so I didn't need to convince them of that. However, they were not satisfied with a single use case, so they started expanding the project to other use cases. They also needed some actionable insights based on the AI solution to reduce the total loss rooted in the charge-off cases. For example, they wanted us to determine the most important factor for customers to get charge-off. That helps the finance enterprise adjust its financial services and reduce the total loss due to the charge-off. We offered this through Explainable AI tools that we had: (a) feature importance, (b) partial dependence plot, and (c) subpopulation analysis. You can read more about these tools in Chapter 18.

— Multiple Use Case: End-to-End Business Solution

As said above, the finance enterprise wanted to go beyond the "charge-off prediction" use case and, for example, predict "the chance of self-correction" as well. Why? Because they didn't have enough resources to dedicate to the collection processes for all the potential cases. If customers most likely would correct their behaviors, the company prefers not to intervene. Do you think that they stopped here? No.

They told me, "Let's say we find out whether customers would self-correct. For those who wouldn't self-correct, how should we intervene?" So, now the question is, what is "the most effective intervention" for the collection team to have a maximum ROI? Do they only need to send emails or mail to those customers in danger of charge-off? Or does the collection team need to be involved further? These are the questions that they need to answer for their daily activities.

After many back-and-forth discussions with the client, we agreed on a list of use cases: [1] detect charge-off cases (classification), [2] estimate the amount of loss (estimation), [3] determine self-correction likelihood (prioritization), and [4] determine the most effective intervention (personalization). These use cases work perfectly in a chain and generate tangible value for the business. This was how we convinced them to sign a contract with us.

 There is one common challenging demand across every enterprise: an end-to-end business solution with actionable and prescriptive insights through a chain of use cases.

The Last Words.

After we defined the chain of values around the charge-off use case for the enterprise client, they agreed to sign a contract with us. This was just the starting point, though. We still had to answer many other questions, such as "Do we have access to the relevant data for each use case in the chain of values?" or "Do we have records of intervention strategies (mail solicitation, settlement offer, or litigation) in past charge-off cases?" Most finance enterprises have large structured datasets that are helpful but not necessarily enough for all the use cases.

Part 2: Data, Data, Data

CHAPTER 7

How to Create a Perfect Data Strategy

N owadays, data has become a strategic resource for companies. Companies aim to build AI solutions using their data to increase their profits. However, since they often do not have perfect data strategies, they fail in their mission. To create a data strategy, you must first understand what a data strategy is. Then, you must create a plan tailored to your company, considering your limitations and capabilities.

A data strategy has four main pillars: Value, Collection, Architecture, and Governance. Through my professional work, I have seen common mistakes repeated across companies as they have sought to create data strategies. In this chapter, I want to use real-world scenarios to describe the best practices for building a data strategy and explain some of the key lessons I have learned in my career thus far.

Value.

The data strategy must describe how data can generate business value in your organization. There are two main ways: (a) building a data-based product or service (external products) and (b) creating reports and gaining insights (internal products). The data strategy must be aligned with your corporate strategy (specifically with your digitalization strategy) and cannot be pursued on a standalone basis. That is why business owners must determine and approve it; otherwise, it will never go beyond the infancy stage.

You can build a data-based product or service that expands your revenue streams. For example, a company that builds an email designer can add a data-based recommender system for its customers to create emails more easily or, better yet, make them more engaging. You can also use data to gain insights and produce reports to enhance current business processes. For instance, a food company can use data-driven reports to measure the quality of its products during the sorting phase. This will help the company improve the efficiency of its processes.

There are two main ways to create value out of data: (a) building a data-based product or service (external products) and (b) creating reports and gaining insights (internal products).

Does a Specific AI Solution Create Business Value?

For artificial intelligence to work, an organization must first identify a business objective that can be served well by an AI solution. For example, a gigantic grocery chain can analyze customer loyalty programs, supply chains, transactions, and foot traffic data. The question for the organization is: Which business objective can be dramatically enhanced using an AI solution? It is common for an organization to start building an AI solution even if its cost-benefit analysis does not make sense. A failure may then stop that organization from pursuing other promising paths. Thus, running a cost-benefit or Expectation vs. Complexity analysis is highly recommended before targeting a business objective using artificial intelligence. Chapter 2 includes some commentary about Expectation vs. Complexity analysis.

Collection.

Let me start with an example. You want to scrape the Rotten Tomatoes website and collect data. You run the web scraper for a day, and the day after, you find another data field that should have been recorded. The process must be repeated. Have you experienced a similar scenario? This can happen in a large-scale data collection, and it will hurt. A large-scale data collection is an expensive process; hence, before conducting it, you must answer critical questions such as: (a) What data fields need to be recorded? (b) How should the data quality be measured? and (c) What is the most scalable way of collecting clean data?

The quality of your data is a significant factor in whether the implementation of your data strategy will be successful or not. That is why a common nightmare among data scientists is to collect a large amount of low-quality data with no use. According to a *Harvard Business Review* article published in 2017, only 3% of data that existed in companies met basic quality standards. Therefore, it is highly recommended not to collect data, at least on a large scale, without knowing how to measure the data quality. Plus, you should not raise your hopes too much regarding your existing data unless its quality meets your basic requirements.

Is the Collected Data Relevant to the Problem at Hand?

Those who are not experts in AI believe that if a vast amount of data is fed into an AI solution, it will be enough, and, just like "magic," AI will do the rest. Wrong! It is correct to assume (with some consideration) that an AI solution will not work if there is not a vast amount of data or if a variety of data types do not exist. However, the relevancy between your data and the problem you are trying to solve cannot be neglected either. Domain experts can identify the relevancy of data to their particular business objectives. They know what is behind the problem they are facing and have a sufficient understanding of their area of expertise to determine the relevant data that needs to be collected. Nevertheless, their opinions can sometimes be undermined while developing an AI solution.

To read more about challenges in large-scale data collection, please continue to Chapter 8.

Tip

You must have a detailed plan before undertaking data collection. It should answer important questions such as "How do you want to use the data?", "What exact data is needed to achieve your goals?", and "How do you measure the data quality?"

Architecture.

The data architecture has two main stages - storage and analysis - with differing requirements for each stage. For example, you must create a data pipeline to ingest and store data quickly with minimal redundancy. NoSQL databases are primarily used for this first stage due to how fast they ingest and store new data. They are also human-readable, which helps you to understand the data. Then, you must create a pipeline to retrieve and analyze the data. SQL databases are often used in this stage because the standard ML libraries, such as scikit-learn, function efficiently with tabular data. Plus, SQL data retrieval is faster than those in NoSQL databases, which is critical in processing big data. When designing data architecture, you must always consider scalability and efficiency. If you could not design the best data architecture in your initial attempt, do be open to revising it as needed since underperforming data architecture will hit you hard down the road.

How Efficiently are Datasets Designed for Use, Scale, and Ease of Maintenance?

As AI projects switch from single-type data to multimodal data, the data architecture becomes even more critical. Together with that, in recent years, data sets have grown exponentially in size and use. This exponential growth causes scalability issues that must be addressed in the data architecture. Last but not least, the data architecture significantly affects the performance and pace of the development of your AI project. Therefore, you will encounter large-scale technical challenges if you do not build a high-performing data architecture.

Once, I was consulting with a large chip manufacturer to build an AI solution to detect the failure rates of its chips. They gave me a large number of datasets, but they each held identical data and contained only one or two useful data fields. Unfortunately, these datasets were also being updated frequently. Their low-quality data architecture led me to spend considerable time creating a dataset that was not just clean and reliable but also easily monitored as it evolved.

 If you do not build a high-performing data architecture, you will encounter large-scale technical challenges, especially when dealing with multimodal or huge datasets.

Governance.

Data governance refers to organizations' processes to manage their data's availability, usability, integrity, and security. At first glance, you might think that governance is not that important; however, many unresolvable issues can be rooted in this final pillar of a data strategy. For example, when commencing a data science project, the ownership of the data is one of the significant issues for an organization to define. Effective data governance also ensures that your data is consistent and trustworthy and does not get misused. You must also take into account that the speed of the development of your data science project may be significantly lowered since issues surrounding data governance can lead to conflicts within an organization. Accordingly, organizations must constantly upgrade their internal policies to comply with existing and new data privacy rules while concurrently striving to expedite the development of the project(s) they are working on.

Is the Required Data Accessible to Various Teams?

In large organizations, since teams often work in silos, many challenges can arise in the collecting and sharing of data. For instance, the database team will be in charge of creating infrastructure for data storage and retrieval, while the AI team will be in charge of analyzing and processing the data. The AI team may have database requirements that the corresponding team does not provide. At the same time, technicians may collect data in the field without the AI and database teams being present or, at the very least, being consulted in advance. In many large organizations, teams do not interact much with each other, and they are thus unaware of each other's difficulties and obstacles. The AI team may perhaps ask for important missing data to improve the performance of the AI model, but the data team will not collaborate to collect that data. Or, perhaps a department will own a valuable dataset that, for technical or political reasons, they will not share with other teams. These are all real problems that impact the work being conducted. An excellent data strategy must allow an organization's various teams to both have access to all required data and to be able to collect new sets of data whenever it is deemed necessary.

A great data strategy must allow an organization's various teams to both have access to all required data and to be able to have new sets of data collected whenever it is deemed necessary.

CHAPTER 8

Significant Issues Connected with Large-Scale Data Collection

I f you are a data scientist or an AI executive, this sentence should be familiar to you: We need more data to build a better AI model.

Although this is a factual statement, it must be used with caution. Before collecting large-scale data, you must answer several vital questions such as "How confident am I that new data will improve model performance?" and "How can I gain more confidence about the quality of newly recorded data?"

Since large-scale data collection is expensive, you must ensure a solid plan before conducting it. For example, if your AI team cannot take advantage of newly recorded data in a reasonable time frame, company dynamics may be affected, and conflict may arise.

In this chapter, I share what I have learned from my experiences over the years and how those experiences have enabled me to conduct large-scale data collection with much more confidence than I could in the early days of my career in AI.

The Performance Analysis Must Validate The Lack Of Data.

An AI model may underperform for reasons other than the volume of training data. For instance, the model's performance may come up short due to underfitting. In addition, your model may not achieve the desired performance because it has not been trained appropriately. The results will not be satisfactory if the learning algorithm fails to converge in the training process.

In what follows, I explain how to recognize when model performance may be improved by including new data in your training data. I also suggest experimenting with your training data to help you identify whether or not it is necessary to record a new dataset.

> Before conducting large-scale data collection, do ensure that your model does overfit the existing data. If so, your model is ready to take advantage of new data.

Using a uniform sampling technique, you can split any reasonable training data into several equally sized buckets. A series of models must be trained using one, two, and all of these buckets. An incremental improvement in model performance needs to be observed when you add the new buckets to the initial bucket. If you do not observe the incremental improvement, the model training process may suffer from an issue, such as model overfit or data quality. In these circumstances, you should rethink (and redo) the entire process after appropriate modification.

If, however, there is an incremental improvement in model performance when the remaining buckets are added to the training data, the model does not yet overfit. In other words, everything is in place to allow you to collect a new set of data. If you detect a fluctuation in model performance while adding the final buckets, you can hypothesize that adding a new dataset may not improve model performance.

Based on my own experiences, this is a necessary type of experimentation before pursuing large-scale data collection.

Data Quality Must Be Defined Early In The Process.

A common adage in artificial intelligence is "garbage in, garbage out." That is why a common nightmare among data scientists is collecting many low-quality and useless data. You should not collect data, at least on a large scale, without knowing how to measure data quality.

Data quality refers to factors such as the quality of labels and recordings. For example, label quality is apt to be fairly poor if the work is done by an inexperienced annotator. Recording quality can also be easily compromised by environmental factors or if the recording device itself is not working properly.

 In order to avoid a "garbage in, garbage out" scenario, you need to define data quality early in the process and then be prepared to record data quality on a large scale.

Although measuring data quality with a quantitative score is helpful, a qualitative score is also advantageous and will save you both time and energy. For example, suppose you measure a heart rate signal using a wristband during the data collection. In that case, you should also measure the skin conductivity level by whatever means are available to you. If you cannot measure the skin conductivity level, you should ensure that you at least record whether or not the individual has a skin "condition" such as tattoo(s) that could affect skin conductivity.

In some cases, you cannot measure and record data quality on a large scale. You might then choose to do data cleaning using outlier detection methods, which will help you exclude outliers from the training data. Here, outliers refer to rare cases, i.e., data points "so far out there" or likely unreliable.

The List Of Required Fields Of Data Must Be Identified.

I want to begin this section with an example. You plan to scrape the web to collect some specific data. The web scraper runs for a day, and the following day, you notice that another field of data should have been recorded. Rats! You must then rerun the process. Have you ever experienced such a situation? An error like this that is not noticed for a day or two is apt to be tolerable; however, if such a mistake is made when conducting large-scale data collection, your work will have been a serious waste of time and resources.

Tip

Have a detailed plan for data collection to avoid the "I wish I had collected this field as well" scenario.

To efficiently collect data to solve a problem, you need to correctly define the required fields early on in the process. If you do not, there may very well be considerable delays as you redo the entire data collection process again – and perhaps again and again and again. Many teams have confided to me over the years that they will collect all sorts of data and then, at a later date, consider how they should use it. In all honesty, this type of approach cannot be endorsed at any level. You may take advantage of that data in the future; however, the chances are good that you will also end up in the "I wish I had collected this field as well" scenario.

The Data Must Be Enhanced After The Collection.

The quality of an AI model is as good as the quality of the training data. Since data collection is complicated and costly, you must resolve any data issues that develop during the collection process as promptly as possible. In other words, you must enhance the quality of the training data through some processing techniques before using it in the model training process.

For example, training data may suffer from missing values or an imbalanced structure, ultimately affecting model performance. In what follows, I will try to briefly answer some common questions, such as "How do I handle imbalanced data?" "How do I use augmented data?" and "How do I deal with missing values?" With minor adjustments, the answers can be applied to various data types, including tabular, visual, and textual data.

Be Thoughtful With Imbalanced Data.

If the training data is balanced over different classes, you can train and evaluate an AI model with less consideration. However, if the data is imbalanced, the model may become biased toward the class with many samples. You must select a proper strategy to deal with imbalanced data; otherwise, your results may be misleading.

 In order to handle an imbalanced dataset, use SMOTE to increase the number of data points from minority classes. Do not get your hopes up too much though, as the new data is synthetic anyway.

For example, suppose there is a collection of training data comprised of 1000 data points, with 900 samples from class A and 100

samples from class B. You will no doubt ask yourself: What strategy should be selected to train a fair model that is not biased toward class A? Similar to other dilemmas in artificial intelligence, the answer depends on the performance metric used to evaluate the model. To handle the imbalanced data, you must enhance either the data curation or the model training.

To continue with this example, suppose that the cost of not detecting class B is high (i.e., high recall on class B is expected). In that case, you must oversample data points from class B using a Synthetic Minority Oversampling Technique (SMOTE). The oversampling will help enhance the presence of data points from the minority class. In other scenarios, you could either modify the data curation using undersampling techniques or select AI models that are less sensitive to imbalanced data, such as the Random Forest.

Augmented Data Is Only Helpful To Some Extent.

When the training data size is not large enough, adding augmented or synthetic data to the training data can improve model performance. Augmented data can make the AI model less sensitive to noise or transformed data (e.g., rotation or scale).

Tip

If needed, you can build your model so that mildly perturbed data will not be able to make significant differences to the model's outputs. Use an oversampling technique to expand your training data and then add synthetically generated noise to it.

For example, if you want to build a rotation-invariant model for a computer vision problem, you could add synthetically rotated data to your training data. In addition, if you prefer to develop a model less sensitive to mildly perturbed data, you could add synthetically perturbed data to the training dataset.

Missing Values Must Be Managed With Proven Strategies.

One of the challenges in AI projects is to deal with missing values. Suppose the ratio of missing values to training data size is considerable. In that case, no replacement strategy is recommended because you have no choice but to drop the feature with many missing values. However, if there are a few missing values, you can replace them based on a proper strategy. That will help you improve model performance without being too strict about the data quality.

- Strategy I (Blind)
  A simple strategy, which is not recommended, is to replace the missing values of a feature with (a) an average of the other data points or (b) a randomly sampled value from the approximate distribution of the same feature. This is a blind strategy and is better than nothing. Using this approach still allows for the preservation of the impaired data.
- Strategy II (Advanced)
  A more sophisticated strategy is to replace the missing values with an average of a selected group of data points. For example, to replace the missing values of feature A, you should first find another feature correlated with feature A, which I will call feature B. Then, you can replace the missing values of feature A with an average of a small group of data points in feature A so that their corresponding values in feature B are in an adjacent neighborhood.

Tip If the number of missing values is not considerable, you can replace them with synthetic data. Again though, do not get your hopes up too much, as the new data is synthetic anyway.

The Last Words.

To collect large-scale data, you must first have a workable and viable plan. For instance, you may surmise using more data will improve your model's performance. You must also be sure how to preserve and record your data quality to avoid a "garbage in, garbage out" scenario. You must also always be confident about the data types you must collect.

In general, I suggest conducting data collection in an iterative form. The iterative approach provides many opportunities to identify unknowns and update data collection plans. Do not forget that once your data collection is concluded, you will still need to investigate and enhance your data. For example, you will still have to deal with missing values and imbalanced data.

Lastly, and very importantly, always remember that having more data may not fix everything.

CHAPTER 9

Feature Selection: Exhaustive vs. Cherry-Picked

There is a philosophical dilemma in data science. What feature selection approach should we use: cherry-picked or exhaustive? The answer is, "It depends." Here, "cherry-picked" means selecting a small set of meaningful features that can be explained very well; "exhaustive" means selecting all possible combinations of the features in the dataset. I come from the tribe of ML experts who believe over-complexity does not help, at least in most cases. Having stated that you may conclude that I always prefer the cherry-picked approach. That is not completely true either, though. I want to compare these two feature selection approaches in this chapter and help you decide when to use each. I will explain their differences over several scenarios to help you identify how to choose the best feature selection approach for your project.

Explainable vs. Unexplainable.

Scenario 1: "You are working on a data science project in a large enterprise. Your managers and other stakeholders lack deep knowledge about machine learning and its potential. Not only did they ask you to create value through this project, but they also asked you to convince them that the solution you settled on is the optimum one. You are frustrated since they do not understand what you are suggesting."

If you use explainable features, i.e., those that the physics of the problem can support, you can more easily gain the trust of your managers and other stakeholders in the project. That does not mean, however, that you should never apply exhaustive feature selection techniques to your project. For this scenario, let's assume that although the entire ML pipeline is not ready, you still must present preliminary results to your managers. If you select and use explainable features rooted in the physics of the problem, you will be more apt to support the specific proposals you are making. Plus, in general terms, you will be more apt to be understood by your audience. So, when faced with a set of circumstances similar to what is described in Scenario 1, I recommend starting with the cherry-picked feature selection approach.

> If you select and use explainable features that are rooted in the physics of the problem, you will be more apt to be able to support the specific proposals that you are making plus, in general terms, you will be more apt to be understood by your audience.

Early Stage vs. Late Stage.

Scenario 2: "You are working for an early-stage startup company. Too many deadlines are being imposed on you, and you have been asked to demonstrate a certain ML model to investors (or, if it is more relevant to your work, you can imagine that you have instead been asked to demonstrate your model in competitions). Fortunately, the expectation for the model performance is not high yet, and any functional ML model will be appreciated."

You may think that in this scenario, an exhaustive approach is better since you do not have time to cherry-pick a small but important set of features for the project. I disagree! Especially in the early days, you will need a plethora of quick fixes to deal with various situations. An exhaustive approach does not give you enough visibility into the process. Therefore, you cannot respond rapidly to unexpected situations that often arise during the early stages of product development. So, I thus recommend the cherry-picked feature selection approach for the early stages and the exhaustive feature selection approach for the late stages of development.

 An exhaustive approach during the early stages of product development does not give you enough visibility into the process and, therefore, you cannot respond rapidly to unexpected situations.

Insight-Oriented vs. Result-Oriented.

Scenario 3: "The main objective of the data science project you are working on is to build insight into the problem being studied. The outcome of the ML model matters, but, more importantly, you must provide suggestions to enhance the processes you are analyzing. Your performance in this scenario is not being measured by the numeric results of the ML model. Instead, you are in charge of creating a list of suggestions, backed by the ML model, that will improve the business logic and processes."

For instance, let's assume you are working on an ML model that will predict the rate of return in a manufacturing process. The process is so complex that no one has sufficient visibility into it. Accordingly, you do not want to add more complexity to it. Your job is to help business owners gain more insight into their manufacturing process by creating a list of actionable tips. The cherry-picked feature selection approach is therefore recommended due to its visibility. The ML pipeline has enough complexity in other places that you should not intentionally add more complexity.

	If the main objective of the data science project you are working on is to build insight into the problem being studied, the cherry-picked feature selection approach is recommended.
Tip	

Takeaway.

In short, in my opinion, you must always start with the cherry-picked feature selection approach when targeting a data science project. Then, when you (a) gain insight into the problem, (b) build trust with your managers and stakeholders, and (c) develop a solid ML pipeline, you can switch to the exhaustive feature selection approach. The exhaustive approach in feature selection allows you to push the model's performance as far as the data permits.

CHAPTER 10

Four Common Mistakes to Avoid When Building an ML Product

A s referenced previously, I once led the AI team at a wearable technology company. The company aimed to build a gesture control armband to let users control their surroundings using hand movements. We developed a gesture recognition engine that used muscle signals as inputs to recognize hand movements.

We had to evaluate an extensive list of ML models before building our industry-grade ML product. We, therefore, created our own "Experiment Management System," i.e., a pipeline that systematically administered all the development steps required to build an ML product, including data collection, model training, model evaluation, and model selection. External experiment management systems (or EMS tools) did not exist at the time, so we had to build everything from scratch (and that ensured that everything was specifically tailored to our needs). In Chapter 17, you will find further commentary regarding experiment management systems.

Ultimately, we built and shipped an ML product to over 100,000 users worldwide. We would never have accomplished this without implementing best practices in its development. This experience helped me learn much about managing the development and building of successful ML products.

In what follows, I share four common mistakes you should avoid when building an ML product and some suggestions for working around them. These four issues have arisen in many projects I have worked on over the years.

A Single End-To-End Model Is Awesome But May Not Exist.

While building an ML product, one significant mistake is insisting on a single end-to-end model to address all scenarios. An ML product can seldom be developed and shipped via a single ML model because use cases often have more variances than you may have initially expected. For example, the ML model used to detect "Hello, Siri" on your iPhone differs from the one used to detect what you say afterward.

 I can build a single end-to-end ML model that will address each and every use case imaginable.

In the early days of the wearable technology project that I led, we aimed to build a gesture recognition model that would serve seven billion people worldwide. It would be an understatement to say that it did work out as well as we intended. It did not take long before we began considering raw muscle signals to obtain better insight into what we were attempting to accomplish.

We discovered that the expected patterns or features for each gesture were inconsistent among users. To put it into simpler words, we learned that individuals are inconsistent and that a single ML model would probably (dare I say, definitely!) not work for everyone. For example, we found different muscle anatomy, skin conductivity, perspiration rates, forearm perimeters, and gesture styles among individuals. These distinctions caused, for instance, gesture A of one person to have a different muscle pattern than gesture A of another person. In addition, and more importantly, we learned that the patterns of gesture A in one individual might be very similar to the patterns of gesture B in another individual. We were left with the task of finding an alternative solution.

We could have assigned individuals into similar assemblies, for example, based on their forearm perimeters, and built a specific model for each group. Although this tactic would probably have improved model performance, it would not have created the desired user experience. After much research and investigation, we thought it best to create two options for our users: a "population model" built by us (the company), which made use of our training dataset, and a "personalized model" built by the users through their data. We let the users themselves decide which model most complemented their needs.

A Blindly Collected Test Dataset Can Be Misleading.

We had to, of course, evaluate the performance of the ML model before each release. Therefore, collecting a valid test dataset early in the process was essential. It almost goes without saying that a valid test dataset must accurately represent user data. For us, our users were not distinguished well enough during the early days of our project. We did not know how, where, or by whom our product would be used. We doubted whether the test dataset would accurately represent user data. To deal with this problem, we utilized two tactics.

 I do not have time to carefully design the data collection protocols. I will spend my time training a complex model.

First, we identified those differences among users that highly affected the model performance. Our analysis indicated that these differences included parameters such as "forearm perimeter" and "skin condition." We could measure the forearm perimeters of individuals in scale, but it was challenging to measure their differences in skin conditions. As a result, and to ensure we were not biased toward any specific group of users, we collected normally distributed data regarding forearm perimeters. Nevertheless, for skin conditions, all we were able to do was use a conductivity meter to measure the skin conditions of a small group of consumers for analysis purposes only (and nothing more).

To reiterate, we were not aware of the distribution of forearm perimeters or skin conditions in our users. If we had had a large number of users, we could have assumed that each variable held a normal distribution. However, we did not have that many users at that time. Accordingly, we were certain that the distribution was definitely skewed. As we knew that our training dataset was not a good representation of our users, we were left merely being able to guesstimate how a new release would affect the user experience. We, therefore, also made use of another tactic. Since we could not be entirely certain about the quality of the releases, we archived all the models and were able to easily roll back to a better previous model if our most recent model did not perform as expected.

Standard Performance Metrics Are Not Always Sufficient.

An academic two-class machine learning problem can be evaluated with standard metrics such as accuracy, precision, and recall. However, an ML product cannot be evaluated so easily. For example, an ML product is often a multi-class problem or requires problem-specific configurations, each of which introduces some complexities to the evaluation framework. A common mistake in building an ML product is to evaluate an ML product with standard performance metrics.

> **Mistake**   I do not need problem-specific metrics. I can use standard performance metrics to evaluate an ML product.

We designed an ML model to identify five hand gestures, i.e., Left, Right, Fist, Spread, and Snap. We evaluated each model's performance in the five classes with three standard parameters, i.e., accuracy, precision, and recall. We, therefore, had 15 (3×5) performance metrics to consider. These 15 parameters were not equally important. For instance, the false positive in class Fist or Snap had different consequences on the user experience across different use cases, and use cases themselves had their own particular requirements. In short, given the complexities, we had to create problem-specific metrics to ensure we were releasing not just a new but also an improved ML model.

More Data Does Not Guarantee Better Results.

"If we collect more data, our model becomes better." You have likely heard this statement many times. However, the reality is that a model's performance does not necessarily improve when feeding more data. Hence, you must archive the models and their performance reports in a library for future purposes. For example, you may want to retrieve them later to conduct a comparative analysis or to deploy them in production. As an aside, Chapter 8 discusses strategies to become more confident in collecting large-scale data.

To build an ML product, you will, at times, build ML models that end up not improving upon the previous model's performance. Nevertheless, you must get into the habit of storing every single model you build and its imperative metadata, such as performance metrics and hyperparameters. Model storage or archiving will help you to run a deeper analysis of the results. In addition, ensure you store all training and testing data next to models in case you need to reproduce the previous experiments. Chapter 17 introduces different experiment management systems to help you better manage the model training process.

Mistake I do not need to archive the ML models. If I collect more data, the model becomes better. Why should I spend time creating an infrastructure?

You can build a library of models in a cloud storage solution such as Amazon S3, a universal artifact management solution such as JFrog, or in compartments provided by a continuous integration solution such as CircleCI. A common practice is to use an artifact management solution that creates better access to the list of stored ML models. You may want, for example, to search through this collection using a query on performance, but you will not be able to do this if your models are being stored in a file-based storage system such as Amazon S3. Experiment management solutions, described in Chapter 17, are the best tools to archive ML models.

Imagine you are an AI lead at a company. During the past several months, you have struggled to design an ML model that fulfills a list of requirements. The deadline comes, and without prior notice to you, the company instead needs an ML model that meets different requirements. You do not have time to do the training and testing again. What can you do? You can query the model library and extract the model with the closest performance to the new requirements.

Could you have responded to this situation if you did not have this collection ready?

Takeaways.

- Have an alternative strategy in place if a single end-to-end ML model does not work. Most of the time, it will not.
- Ensure test data is an accurate representation of user data.
- Build a library of models and tag them with useful metadata. They certainly will be needed in the process.
- Use problem-specific metrics to evaluate end-to-end performance. Standard performance metrics will not suffice.

CHAPTER 11

How to Improve Data Quality in RAG Systems

Retrieval-augmented generation (RAG) is an effective method for answering queries by leveraging contextual data that is not included in the model's training data. This method is often used when the resources are unfit for model training, such as rapidly changing enterprise documents requiring high privacy. This method also decreases the chance of hallucination by narrowing the response context. RAG has several steps, including document indexing, information retrieval, and response generation. The information retrieval step aims to extract focused context or potential responses from resources before passing them to the response generator. In this chapter, I highlight query transformation techniques designed for information retrieval that improve RAG performance.

User queries often lack precise descriptions or language correctness. Plus, there is no guarantee that user queries match the wording of the resources. These differences impact retrieval quality, which can't be resolved by any LLM in the response generation step. On another note, LLMs likely make mistakes when they aim to respond to a complex query in one step. We need to break down the original query into several sub-queries before aiming to answer the original query. These challenges can be addressed by a family of techniques named "query transformation," which improves the quality of input data in RAG solutions.

We use various techniques daily to better understand a question (simple or complex) and respond more effectively. For example, we use techniques to expand discussion perspectives, break down complex questions, and define template responses. Similarly, we can use these techniques to let machines answer questions better through more effective information retrieval. Several techniques were previously introduced to implement these techniques in advanced RAG systems, such as (1) query refinement, (2) query expansion, and (3) query decomposition. For the best performance, you should implement these techniques with extremely large language models such as GPT4 or Llama3 450B .

Most of the usual concerns around LLMs, such as privacy or cost, don't apply to question transformation since, for example, questions often don't include factual information. However, if you have restrictions on using those LLMs, you should use fined-tuned instruction-following LLMs to implement question transformation techniques. Below, I provided prompts that are tuned for GPT4.

Query Refinement

Query refinement is a technique to improve the clarity of the original query by rewriting it to different potential forms using the context. It also corrects potential spelling or grammatical errors.

Users interacting with natural language interfaces don't follow any rules or guidelines. They just write whatever comes into their mind, which may (and will) include spelling and grammatical errors and lack enough details. Refinement helps the query become much clearer and machine-understandable.

```
prompt = """Given the context of each text, rewrite the following
text into a well-structured question by choosing the most likely
type of sentence (declarative, interrogative, imperative,
exclamatory). Feel free to use extra words or even synonyms to
enhance the text. Do this 3 times with different words but the
same structure. Don't use polite words.

Text = serial numbers Emerson valves after 2020 high-
pressure"""
```

```
Query:
"serial numbrs Emerson valves after 2020 high-presure"

Transformed (Refined) Qery:
1- Which serial numbers are used for Emerson high-pressure
valves produced after 2020?
2- What are the serial numbers for Emerson valves that handle
high pressure and were made post-2020?
3- Identify the serial numbers for Emerson valves manufactured
after 2020 that are designed for high pressure.
```

Query Expansion

Query expansion is a technique to broaden perspectives by adding extra details or sample responses to the original query.

Here, I want to highlight two common query expansion techniques: query2doc and HyDE. In query2doc, the original query is concatenated with the pseudo-documents generated by LLMs in response to the original query. The pseudo-documents often contain highly relevant information to aid query disambiguation and guide retrieval. Similarly, HyDE uses LLMs to generate hypothetical documents in response to a query with one small difference. In HyDE, we don't concatenate the document with the original query. We purely use the hypothetical document for retrieval.

Note that pseudo or hypothetical documents refer to the same concept with different terminology. In both techniques, we first generate documents that, although they may not answer the query, serve as a valuable example of a reasonable response. You can find a sample prompt to implement the query expansion below. If you want to use HyDE, you can use the native implementation of HyDE in the Llamaindex framework.

```
prompt = """Given the context of each text, rewrite the following
text into a well-structured question by choosing the most likely
type   of   sentence   (declarative,   interrogative,   imperative,
exclamatory). Feel free to use extra words or even synonyms to
enhance the text. Do this 3 times with different words but the
same structure. Don't use polite words.

Text = serial numbers Emerson valves after 2020 high-
pressure"""
```

Query:
"How can one identify a malfunctioned high-pressure Emerson
valve?"

Transformed (Expanded) Qery:
To identify a malfunctioning high-pressure Emerson valve, start
by observing any unusual behavior such as erratic operation,
inconsistent pressure readings,or unusual noises. Check for leaks
around the valve body or connections, as these can indicate seal
or fitting issues. Additionally, monitor the valve's response to
control signals; if it fails to open or close properly or does
not maintain the set pressure, it may be malfunctioning. Conduct
a visual inspection for any signs of physical damage or wear.
Finally, consult the valve's diagnostic tools or software if
available,   as   these   can   provide   detailed   error   codes   or
performance data. If these checks indicate issues, it may be
necessary to perform further diagnostic tests or contact Emerson
for technical support.

Query Decomposition

Query decomposition is a technique for breaking down complex
queries into simpler sub-queries. The results of these sub-queries are
then combined to generate the final response.

In real-world use cases, RAG pipelines must effectively respond to
complex queries with multiple aspects, which also need some level of
reasoning. In this case, we must break down these queries into simpler
ones, allowing the solution to extract answers more targeted and
efficiently. Each question may need to be answered using different
resources, such as an SQL database or a collection of documents. This

approach leads to more accurate answers. Let me give you an example.

```
prompt = """Break down a complex question into a list of sub-
questions that help answer the main question. Break down the
original question minimally as needed. Keep answer concise and
limit only to the list of sub-questions.

Question - Extract the serial numbers of Emerson valves built
after 2020 designed for high-pressure scenarios and comply with
API 6A."""
```

```
Query:
"Extract the serial numbers of Emerson valves built after 2020
designed for high-pressure scenarios and comply with API 6A."

Transformed (Decomposed) Qery:

- What are the serial numbers of Emerson valves built after 2020?
- Which of these valves are designed for high-pressure scenarios?
- Which of the high-pressure valves comply with API 6A standards?
```

The Last Words.

You can improve the data quality and optimize information retrieval using query transformation techniques in the pre-retrieval stage. You can also re-evaluate the retrieved documents in the post-retrieval stage using query-document relevancy techniques such as BM25 or ReRank. Enhancing a RAG solution requires more than query transformation in the real world. In this chapter, I highlighted the most common query transformation techniques used in the industry. However, there are more techniques. You can check out the query transformation cookbook created by Llamaindex.

Part 3: Building an Effective AI Solution

CHAPTER 12

Deep Learning in Simple Words

H ere, I want to use simple words to explain deep learning, one of the AI methodologies that significantly impact the field of artificial intelligence. This may help you answer questions such as "What is deep learning?" and "Why does deep learning work?" I have tried to share my understanding of deep learning so that you can comprehend the big picture. Once you understand and recognize the big picture, many of the questions you have in the back of your mind will hopefully be resolved. After reading this chapter, you will be familiar with a technology that revolutionized this field.

Where Did The Story Start?

There are two main steps in the conventional machine learning workflow: (1) "feature extraction" and (2) "model building". In the feature extraction step, we aim to represent data in a numerical space (also referred to as a feature space). In the model-building step, we strive to design a computerized engine to, for example, determine the group to which each data point belongs. If you can create a model to classify data within the feature space seamlessly, it means that feature extraction and classification work together in the manner they are expected to. Nevertheless, the story is not always as simple as you may suspect.

Feature Extraction Is Always Challenging.

For a long time, AI experts have had to work with domain specialists to extract features for each problem. They had to be creative and collaborate to realize this goal. This process was intricate and non-transferable across projects. Plus, handcrafted feature extraction was nearly impossible in some applications due to the complexity of the problems being worked on.

For example, in face recognition, challenges such as variation in illumination, occlusion, and deformation could not be handled individually through handcrafted feature extraction. Therefore, everyone was interested in finding a methodology that replaced handcrafted feature extraction with a data-driven approach.

Tough Problems Need More Complex Models.

First, allow me to define a machine learning model. A machine learning model is a mathematical function that takes data and, for example, spits out a result displaying the group a data point belongs to or the estimated value of a target variable. This mathematical function contains a list of unknown parameters that must be estimated or trained to ensure that its output can determine each data point's membership group.

The number of parameters in a model represents the model's complexity. In theory, a model with a myriad of parameters is more powerful and thus more preferred than a model with a few parameters, but only if you can tune its parameters by successfully using classic methods. Nonetheless, when the number of parameters increases, other challenges ensue.

> A model with many parameters is more powerful and thus more preferred than a model with a few parameters, but only if you can tune its parameters by successfully using classic methods.

- Does adding complexity to the network help?

If you want to find out how configuration parameters such as learning rate, activation function, or architecture affect the outcome of a neural network, I highly recommend checking out TensorFlow's interactive demo Playground.

What Is Deep Learning?

Deep learning is a series of machine learning methods based on special architectures of deep neural networks (neural networks with many hidden layers) that can conduct both feature extraction and classification in unison and with little human effort. Deep neural networks cannot be considered deep learning without a special architecture. They are much more advanced than layers, which are simply fully connected. The special architectures are mainly built upon a concept named "capsule." A capsule is a group of neurons in each layer that do a lot of internal computation and output a compact result representing a data property such as Convolution. In this chapter, I explain why special architecture changes the game in favor of deep learning.

A Success Story: AlphaGo

AlphaGo project created by Deepmind is one of the success stories of deep learning. As stated by Deepmind: "AlphaGo is the first computer program to defeat a Go world champion." First, let me describe why Go is special.

Go is the most challenging classic game to be targeted by artificial intelligence. Why? Primarily due to the number of moves a player can choose. After the first two moves, there are about 130,000 moves in Go. This number is at 400 possible moves in chess. You can see that the search space in Go is unarguably vast. Deep learning can be a good choice when the search space is drastically vast.

Another reason deep learning is the right method to target Go is that it is rooted in how Go is played. If you ask Go players how they decide on a move, they often tell you it just felt right. In these scenarios, when you can not define features, you can not use classical machine learning algorithms. Deep learning can be a good choice when determining a proper feature set is not feasible.

What Is A Convolutional Neural Network?

A convolutional neural network (or CNN) is a class of deep learning architectures commonly used to analyze images, such as image classification, object detection, and video action recognition. In general, the convolutional neural network is designed to be used with any data that has some spatial invariance in its structure, such as face or speech recognition. Spatial invariance means that, for example, a cat ear in the top left of the image has the same features as a cat ear in the bottom right. CNNs are built upon two main building blocks described below.

- Convolution — CNNs are spatially invariant since they are built upon the convolution operator. Convolution is a mathematical operation that does the integral of the product of two functions (signals), with one of the signals flipped (if needed). In the past, convolution operators have been used, for example, to compute the correlation between two signals or find patterns in signals. This operator functions well for feature extraction in visual data. Much of the progress made in computer vision over the past few years is partly due to convolutional neural networks.
- Pooling — Another building block in CNNs is a pooling layer. Its function is to progressively reduce the spatial size of the data to

reduce the network size and the algorithm sensitivity to the precise position of the feature in the input. The network size translates to the number of weights that must be estimated during the training phase.

You sometimes also need to add extra pixels with pixel_intensity=0 around the boundary of the input images to increase the effective size. That helps to keep image size fixed after applying convolutional layers. This process is called padding.

What Are Some Special Architectures?

- **AlexNet** — AlexNet is a successful implementation of convolutional neural networks that won the ImageNet Large Scale Visual Recognition Challenge (ILSVRC) in 2012. The architecture has been published in NeurIPS 2012 by Alex Krizhevsky, Ilya Sutskever, and Geoffrey Hinton. In this architecture, the input is an RGB image of size 256×256, which was randomly cropped into size 224×224. The architecture contains 650,000 neurons and 60 million parameters. It took 5-6 days to train on two GTX 580 3GB GPUs. It consists of 5 Convolutional Layers and 3 Fully Connected Layers. They used Rectified Linear Units (ReLUs) as activation functions for the first time.

- **VGG16** — A standard way to improve the performance of deep neural networks is by increasing the depth. VGG-16 was invented by folks at the Visual Geometry Group at the University of Oxford. This architecture has 13 convolutional and three fully-connected layers. They also used the ReLU activation function as the tradition carrying over from AlexNet. This network stacks more layers than AlexNet and uses smaller filters (2×2 and 3×3). It consists of 138M parameters.

- **ResNet50** — With the network depth increasing, accuracy gets saturated and degrades rapidly, primarily because we can not train it properly. Microsoft Research addressed this problem with ResNet50 — using skip (or shortcut) connections while building deeper models. A deeper CNN (up to 152 layers) without compromising model generalization. This is an excellent idea.

How To Build A Simple Deep Learning Architecture?

Building a deep learning model involves defining the architecture of the neural network, choosing the right layers, compiling the model with an appropriate loss function and optimizer, and then training the model on your data. You can implement this process with Keras or Pytorch. Keras is a high-level neural network library with a Python interface, primarily running on top of TensorFlow (developed by Google). PyTorch is an open-source deep learning framework developed by Facebook's AI Research Lab (FAIR). Below, you can find a sample implementation of a convolutional neural network using Keras.

```
from keras.models import Sequential
from keras.layers import Dense, Dropout, Flatten
from keras.layers import Conv2D, MaxPooling2D
from keras.optimizers import SGDmodel = Sequential()

model.add(Conv2D(32, (3, 3), activation='relu', input_shape=(100, 100, 3)))
model.add(Conv2D(32, (3, 3), activation='relu'))
model.add(MaxPooling2D(pool_size=(2, 2)))
model.add(Dropout(0.25))

model.add(Conv2D(64, (3, 3), activation='relu'))
model.add(Conv2D(64, (3, 3), activation='relu'))
model.add(MaxPooling2D(pool_size=(2, 2)))
model.add(Dropout(0.25))

model.add(Flatten())
model.add(Dense(256, activation='relu'))
```

```
model.add(Dropout(0.5))
model.add(Dense(10, activation='softmax'))

sgd = SGD(lr=0.01, decay=1e-6, momentum=0.9, nesterov=True)
model.compile(loss='categorical_crossentropy', optimizer=sgd)
model.fit(x_train, y_train, batch_size=32, epochs=10)
```

How To Train A Deep Learning Model?

As described above, training a neural network refers to a process that calculates the weights in the network to minimize the objective function. This is an optimization problem where you must search for the optimum set of weights (or parameters) that minimize the loss function. The efficacy of the search method determines the speed and outcome of the training process.

In general, to implement a search method, you must have answers to the following questions: (1) "How to determine the search direction?" and (2) "How to determine the search step?". The gradient descent technique has been used to guide the search process in training neural networks. The search direction is determined by the gradient operator, and the search step is determined by a hyperparameter λ, which is also called the learning rate. In short, the update mechanism in the gradient descent technique is as follows: $x_m = x_n - \lambda * \nabla f(x_n)$. Classic gradient descent techniques can not be used simply for deep learning techniques, where many weights (parameters) and a number of data points often exist.

Stochastic gradient descent (SGD) is a variation of the gradient descent technique that is more efficient for deep learning models. This method calculates the error and updates the model for each data point in the training dataset, contrary to computing errors using batch data. The SGD is fast in search and offers more frequent model updates. On the other hand, the SGD results are different in each run, and convergence is slower compared to the standard technique.

Instead of using only the gradient of the current step to guide the search, we can use the gradient of the past steps, knowing that the most recent ones are more important. This is called Momentum in the optimization context. Therefore, we can, for example, use an exponential average of the gradient steps for a more efficient search process.

Other techniques exist to solve the optimization problem, such as AdaGrad (Adaptive Gradient) or Adam (Adaptive Moment Estimation). These methods are variations of gradient descent optimization that adaptively change the learning rate to ensure a more efficient search process. Simply put, the learning rate or search step can be different for each direction in the search space and at each moment in time.

Food For Thought — In machine learning algorithms, we choose a metric (e.g., accuracy) to evaluate a model; however, we optimize a different objective function and "hope" that minimizing its value will improve the metric we care about. So, what can we do to ensure that we reach the desired requirements?

Why Does Deep Learning Work Well?

The Special And Modular Architecture Opens Many Doors.

One major drawback of conventional neural networks is the lack of specialized building blocks (a building block is a group of neurons that do considerable internal computation and then output a compact result). Using specialized building blocks whose outputs represent a data property is an essential aspect of deep learning methods. The specialized building blocks make the analysis and training more adaptable to the new training schema and design process. On the other hand, the building block in conventional neural networks is a network layer that does not always create meaningful results. In the end, using specialized building blocks will help you design more complex and trainable neural networks that can then be used to successfully target intricate problems.

A group of deep learning methods specialized for image processing is referred to as a convolutional neural network (or CNN). In these networks, specialized building blocks aim to extract features from images, including edges or shapes. These building blocks, also termed convolutional layers, are similar to their counterpart in conventional image processing, where they are called filters, yet there is a significant difference. In deep learning, these building blocks are designed and trained through an algorithm using the training data, while in conventional techniques, they are designed by a person, usually an engineer. The successful development of AlexNet, a special neural network architecture for image processing, solved one of the challenges that researchers in machine learning had struggled with.

 One of the major drawbacks of conventional neural networks is the lack of meaningful building blocks. Explainability is one of their weak points.

The Linear And Nonlinear Parts Are Well-Separated.

If a machine learning model is nonlinear, you may have difficulty working with it. Nonlinearity generally suggests that it will be tougher to train the model and then analyze the resultant data. That is why, more often than not, the winners in conventional ML models are those consisting of a combination of linear models (precisely, piecewise linear models), such as "Random Forest" and "XGBoost."

An essential part of neural networks is their computation unit, also called a neuron. In brief, a neuron is a mathematical operator that calculates a weighted sum of its incoming data that passes through the activation function. This function can be linear, piecewise linear, and nonlinear.

A neural network is built upon a multitude of neurons that pass information to each other in directions determined by the model architecture. Note that a neural network is a nonlinear function; however, its basis is linear. A neural network's linear and nonlinear parts are well-separated and, therefore, can be managed with little effort.

We Can Now Systematically Train A Complex Model.

A deep neural network can have literally billions of parameters that need to be trained. Experts hesitated to work with such models years ago, but we can effectively train deep neural networks today. Computing power has also become accessible to everyone at lower costs compared to the past. In addition, researchers have introduced new methodologies that allow deep neural networks to be trained systematically.

Second, given that it is such a tedious task, you now do not always need to take the time to train a deep neural network from scratch. You can often start with a network that has previously been trained on millions of data points by another research group or major corporation. You thus only have to fine-tune the network with your data. You can subsequently then freeze parts of the network as it will be ready to perform basic operations such as edge detection in image processing or word vectorization in natural language processing.

Third, as described above, the nonlinear and linear parts of deep learning models are separated. Hence, if the nonlinear parts create an issue in training, you can modify them without affecting the other parts of the model. For example, if you use the sigmoid as an activation function in deep neural networks, the training step will fail. Therefore, without much effort, you can replace that nonlinear function (i.e., the sigmoid function) with a piecewise linear function (i.e., a rectified linear function).

The Last Words.

We sometimes jump into implementing complex algorithms and methodologies while expending less time and resources on learning their high-level concepts. It is indeed wonderful to be able to quickly write code to, for example, calculate document similarity or extract document topics. However, you may be misled if you do not know the underlying details. I have tried to shed some light on deep learning in this chapter. I hope you have found it informative.

CHAPTER 13

The Achilles Heel of AI Methods: Similarity Metrics

When you are measuring the similarity between two objects, including documents or images, important questions will arise, such as "What is the right way of defining similarity?", "How can I measure the similarity?" and "How should I analyze the similarity metric?" I have been fascinated with the similarity concept for a long time; hence, I want to share some insight I have gained through the years. I cannot describe all the details in a book of this size, but I will try to bring as much understanding as possible to this topic.

Tip

If two objects are identical, there is no room for interpretation. However, subjects that are not precisely identical may very well be open to interpretation.

Anything Less Than Being Identical Is Subject To Interpretation.

We, as humans, have a complex system to interpret similarity. Two objects can be similar in one aspect and different in another; at times, that difference will be in the eye of the beholder. The concept of similarity, regardless of how it is measured, varies across contexts and problems. If two objects are alike, there is no room for interpretation. However, subjects that are not precisely identical may very well be open to interpretation. For instance, how similar do you think the images are in Figure 3 below? If the likeness means having similar elements, they are identical; otherwise, they are poles apart. Remember that an object can be a time series, a document, or an image. And the similarity measure can become more sophisticated.

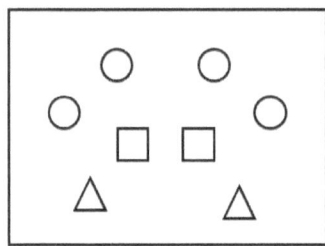 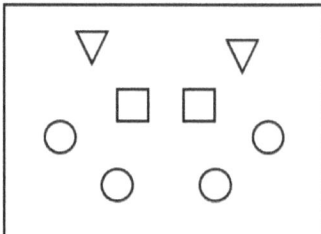

Figure 3- Both images contain similar elements. Are they similar, though?

Every time a decision is made, the human brain will perform a series of data processing steps, such as rotation or translation, based on what is required. Nevertheless, an AI solution cannot perform those data processing steps without being previously programmed and trained. Sometimes, for example, you may need a rotation-invariant algorithm and, at other times, a rotation-variant algorithm. Whatever your requirements are, they must be set in advance.

The "rabbit and duck" illusion, shown in Figure 4 below, is an interesting example. An identical shape with an altered angle can be interpreted differently depending on how you view it. This proves the significance of angle or rotation in the human interpretation of an image. Always be aware of the sensitivity of an algorithm to the angles of the input data.

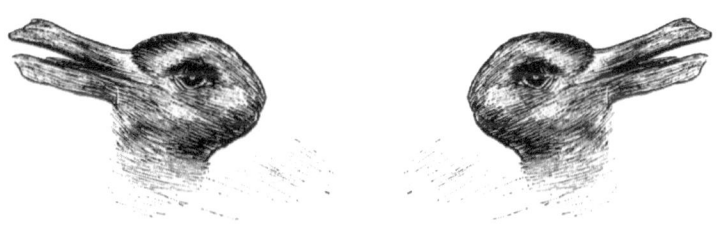

a) Original image b) Rotated image

Figure 4- The rabbit and duck illusion. Source: Wikipedia.

We Compare Objects Based On Different Characteristics.

Unless subjects are precisely identical, they may likely be interpreted in many different ways. The question then to ask is, "What are the main characteristics of the similarity?" If you can elaborate on the likeness aspects to be measured, it will become easier to formulate the similarity metric. (As an aside, since the previous section was explained using image data, this section uses text data to illustrate the high-level concepts that can be applied to any data regardless of its type.)

In text processing, there are three main similarity measures, namely, lexical (form-related), syntactical (structure-related), and semantical (meaning-related). Nonetheless, utilizing any of these measures does not disregard the significance of the others. Two sentences can be similar according to their form but different according to their meaning.

The simplest textual data is a series or string of letters that may or may not have meaning. The similarity between two strings can be measured by diverse metrics, such as whether or not they are string-based (e.g., edit distance) or token-based (e.g., Jaccard distance). The edit distance is the minimum number of operations required to transform one string into the other, and the Jaccard distance is the inverse of the number of characters both strings share compared to (read: divided by) all characters in both strings.

I will not elaborate here on how you must implement these methodologies. I want to emphasize, though, that even the simplest form of similarity, such as string similarity, can be measured differently. The lengthier the data, the more complex the similarity concept.

The Behavior Of Similarity Metrics Must Be Analyzed In Detail.

Complexity arises when you want to measure similarity using a mathematical equation. The former section partially explains the various methods to calculate either the similarity or the distance between two objects. In this section, I wish to describe the consequence of analyzing the similarity metric's behavior regardless of the calculation method.

In general, you can use similarity and distance interchangeably with some consideration. For example, similarity and distance are opposite to each other, so if two objects are similar, it means a small distance separates them. That is why, in many cases, similarity(x,y) = 1 - distance(x,y) or similarity(x,y) = 1 / distance(x,y). These methods impose altered sensitivity to the similarity metric, which becomes crucial while using it in an AI algorithm.

The quality of a similarity metric depends on the dimension of space where the objects are represented. For instance, if the cosine similarity between two objects in a two-dimensional space is 0.9, you may call those points similar. Yet, you may not reach the same conclusion with that threshold in a high-dimensional space.

Tip

You should ensure that the similarity metric: (a) works efficiently in a high-dimensional space and (b) measures the differences as expected.

If $\cos(x,y) = \cos(x,z) = 0.9$, you cannot make a useful conclusion on the relationship of y and z in a high-dimensional space. On the contrary, based on spatial geometry, you can draw valuable conclusions in a two-dimensional space. These observations show that you must consider the space dimension when interpreting the results of cosine similarity.

Moreover, a distance metric may work appropriately in a low-dimensional space but lose its efficiency in a high-dimensional space. Metrics such as edit distance that require dynamic programming underperform in a high-dimensional space due to computational complexity.

Tip

The quality of a similarity metric depends both on the dimension of space where the objects are represented and how the similarity metric is calculated.

The Last Words.

In artificial intelligence, particularly with clustering techniques, you must always work with similarity or distance metrics. For instance, one of the main steps in clustering techniques is to determine the cluster that a new point belongs to. In this scenario, you must calculate the similarity between the new data point and, for example, the cluster centroid and then compare it with the threshold to determine the group to which the data point belongs.

Although you can use Euclidean distance or cosine distance in many different types of applications, it is recommended that you use a distance metric that best suits your specific problem.

If you wish to become an expert in the AI field, you must take the time to study the similarity concept. Mastering the similarity concept will not solve all your problems, but neglecting it will undoubtedly create some challenges. I encourage you to consider it an essential tool in your toolbox.

CHAPTER 14

Word2vec Models are Simple Yet Revolutionary

A major challenge in natural language processing is how to encode text data, such as words or sentences, into high-dimensional vectors. Previously, you would have mostly used encoders such as one-hot, term frequency, or TF-IDF (Term Frequency-Inverse Document Frequency). However, words' semantic and syntactic properties were not captured in these techniques. Word2vec models allow you to encode words in more meaningful ways. Over time, the word2vec model went beyond its original scope and found its way into other AI fields, such as recommender systems and knowledge extraction.

In this chapter, I will describe the word2vec model and its applications. I will also discuss why word2vec models are considered simple but revolutionary. Finally, I will briefly answer some of the most common questions that arise when clustering a dataset with no labels, a method that is widely used on the vectors generated by word2vec models.

Word2vec: Why, What, And How.

Vectors are powerful mathematical tools for representing and organizing data. One of the first steps in building an ML model is data vectorization, which is essential for the downstream tasks in the pipeline. The word2vec model is a well-known ML model used to vectorize text in natural language processing.

When representing data in vector formats, you can use linear algebra tools for various purposes, such as model training and data augmentation. Linear algebra is the mathematics of vector spaces and provides a potent set of tools to, for example, calculate the distance between two vectors or between a point and a hyperplane.

It is relatively easy to compute the distance of a vector from hyperplanes when you represent the data in a vector space. A Support Vector Machine (SVM), a popular and formidable AI model, uses these concepts to locate the hyperplane that best divides a dataset into two classes. It is also quite simple to compute the distance between two vectors using the well-accepted cosine distance metric.

Let me share with you now a successful story of using vectorization in an industry challenge. As I mentioned in the opening pages, I led the AI team at a wearable technology company in the development of a gesture control armband. We successfully built an armband composed of eight sensors that recorded muscle activities at the forearm level. Thus, we had an 8-d vector dataset at each instant. After collecting a literally huge amount of data, we began the process of analyzing it. We spanned the 8-D space into 50+ clusters, each of which was represented by its centroid. While each recording was represented by a centroid (e.g., C1 or C2), a gesture was defined as a back-to-back series of these centroids (e.g., C1C2C2C3C1). Centroids were like "letters," and gestures were like "words." After representing gesture data using the creative format, we started using standard natural language processing techniques to recognize whether a word (you can call it a gesture) had occurred. In this representation, a gesture or word was a series of letters recorded by the armband. The approach was very novel and worked very well for us. Some years later, Facebook purchased the IP of this algorithm from the company.

If you did not beforehand, I hope you now agree with me on the importance of data vectorization, especially a vectorization that maintains the semantics of the data within its geometry.

Tip

Word2vec is a methodology that represents words by numerical vectors spanned in a high-dimensional space, while at the same time also maintaining the semantic and syntactic relationships of the words.

Word2vec refers to a word embedding or encoding methodology published by Mikolov et al. in 2013. It represents words by numerical vectors spanned in a high-dimensional space while maintaining their semantic and syntactic relationships. These vectors are features in natural language processing and machine learning applications.

Two main neural architectures are introduced to compute these vectors: (a) continuous bag-of-words and (b) continuous skip-gram. I do not want to describe the details of these methods here; however, let me shed some light on the capacity of word2vec models.

A representation of complex data while preserving a "specific geometry of data" such as semantic relatedness is a classic approach. For instance, between 2000 and 2010, there was an abundance of interest in manifold learning, with one focus being on introducing techniques such as Isometric Mapping (IsoMap) or Locally Linear Embedding (LLE) to represent images in lower-dimensional spaces while preserving a specific geometry of data. Although these attempts were unfortunately ineffective, their legacies were passed on to word2vec models.

Tip

A word2vec model learns meaningful relationships and encodes that relatedness into vector similarity.

What Are The Main Applications Of Word2vec?

The word2vec model extracts the notion of relatedness across words or products such as semantic relatedness, synonym detection, concept categorization, selectional preferences, and analogy. A word2vec model learns meaningful relationships and encodes that relatedness into vector similarity. The main applications of word2vec can be summarized in knowledge discovery and recommender systems.

Knowledge Discovery.

You can use textual data, such as a series of scientific articles, to effectively train word2vec models to, in part, detect hidden relationships among elements of those articles. For example, in 2019, a study published in *Nature* introduced a novel word2vec model that could discover new chemical compounds with specific properties. They trained their model using over three million abstracts from scientific research articles published across a thousand journals over approximately 100 years. The model helped them to extract relationships and analogies among chemical compounds.

Recommender Systems.

Word2vec models are not limited to textual data; they will work for other data types, such as users' click sessions, search histories, or purchase histories. This method can be utilized to build powerful recommender systems, which can increase online business profits by enhancing both the click-through rate (CTR) and conversions. You can create fixed-sized vector representations that capture human-like relationships and similarities between different items, such as places or products. Airbnb, for instance, trained word2vec models on user click and conversion (the final step in a booking procedure) sessions to create business value. It is important to note that humans do not jump from item to item without having an objective in mind. The items, products, or places a user goes through during a visit to a website are somehow connected to the way they think and act, and a word2vec model can capture that relatedness. I am fascinated by the myriad of practical applications of word2vec models. I hope you find this subject matter as interesting as I do.

Most of the time, a revolutionary solution is the one with innovative problem formulation. As Einstein said, "Make everything as simple as possible, but not simpler."

How Can Word2vec Be Simple Yet Revolutionary?

A revolutionary solution does not need to be complex. Most of the time, a revolutionary solution is one with innovative problem formulation. If you can formulate a problem well, other downstream steps become effortless. As Einstein mused, "Make everything as simple as possible, but not simpler." Word2vec does just that.

In what follows, I explain why word2vec models can be considered simple and revolutionary.

- **Meaningful embedding-** The purpose of word2vec is not strictly word vectorization. Texts were vectorized using other methods before word2vec was introduced in 2013. Word2vec is a methodology that represents words by numerical vectors spanned in a high-dimensional space while also maintaining the semantic and syntactic relationships of the words.

- **Pre-trained libraries-** Many pre-trained word2vec models, ready to download and easy to incorporate, exist. These models open many doors for various NLP tasks, including sentiment analysis and summarization. Large-size pre-trained models such as *word2vec-google-news-300* are the foundations of revolutionary NLP solutions.
- **Contextualized models-** You can train a contextualized word2vec model using open-source code optimized to work efficiently and fast on a specific corpus of data. For example, if the target data is from the world of finance, use a model trained on the finance corpus. Open-source code lets you train a contextualized model for your intended purpose.
- **Standalone usage-** NLP tasks are complicated. Without knowing the details of the initial steps, you cannot design and develop the next steps properly. Do not hesitate to use and analyze standalone word2vec models, providing better insight into the entire ML pipeline. For instance, although no one would ever doubt the capabilities of a BERT model, sentence similarity may work better with a word2vec model.

The Most Common Questions In Clustering.

When clustering a dataset with no labels, various questions will often come to mind, including: "What is the correct number of clusters?" and "What is a good metric to evaluate the clustering performance?" The first question may arise when you work with, for instance, the k-means algorithm, a popular vector quantization method that requires the number of clusters to be specified. As you might guess, the second question can arise when you want to evaluate the final results derived from a clustering technique.

Real-world data, such as vectors generated by a word2vec model, is often high-dimensional, and you will find that the clustering challenges can become more controversial with such high-dimensional data. Therefore, reducing the data dimension to conduct further analysis is often helpful. For instance, you may need to visualize data in a 2-D space to properly analyze clustering results. To do that, you must use dimension reduction techniques such as Principal Component Analysis (PCA) or Locally Linear Embedding. However, it is important to note that the data structure can be altered during the dimension reduction.

Let us assume that the data structure was not significantly altered during the process. Even with this assumption, clustering results in the transformed (i.e., dimension-reduced) space may still differ from those in the original space due to the performance of the distance metric in those spaces. The same clustering algorithm will have been utilized, but a discrepancy will ensue.

You will find that clustering results are sensitive to the space dimension due to the performance of distance metrics (an essential tool in clustering techniques). This behavior is referred to as the curse of dimensionality, a phenomenon that may occur when analyzing data in high-dimensional spaces, but which does not occur in low-dimensional spaces. More information about how to analyze distance or similarity metrics can be found in Chapter 13.

Tip

Clustering results in the transformed space can be quite different from what they were in the original space. The outcome is sensitive to the space dimension.

This section does not explain the math behind the silhouette and elbow methods, two standard methods to determine the optimal number of clusters. You can easily find that information elsewhere. What I would like to do, though, is share my experience working with these methods and provide some hopefully useful insight.

There Is No Correct Number Of Clusters, But There Is An Optimal One.

Let me be candid. There is no correct number of clusters but an optimal one. Should you select, for example, the k-means algorithm for your problem, you will need to run the algorithm for several consecutive k (i.e., the number of clusters). Then, you must compute the clustering performance for each k. You can thus determine the k in a way that works for your problem.

Before doing that, though, you must first select a performance metric that effectively evaluates the clustering quality. Then, you need to run the clustering algorithm with several configurations (for example, the number of clusters) and evaluate each run's performance. Everything necessary to determine the number of clusters will, at that point, become apparent.

Once that is resolved, your next question will presumably be: "What is a good metric to evaluate the clustering performance?" The answer, perhaps not surprisingly, is: "It depends."

Cluster Using Inertia And Evaluate Using The Silhouette.

A clustering algorithm is an optimization problem. The objective function of the optimization problem can vary from the performance metric of the corresponding clustering algorithm. The objective function is used within the optimization process, and the performance metric is used to evaluate the final result.

For instance, the k-means algorithm is designed to cluster data by minimizing the sum of within-cluster variances, also known as inertia. Nevertheless, you may want to use the silhouette coefficient to evaluate the clustering performance. The silhouette coefficient evaluates the final results based on the within-cluster and between-cluster distances.

Although you cannot easily change the objective function in the k-means algorithm due to technical challenges, a different performance metric can be used to evaluate the clustering results. You may be curious why you should not use a similar metric in both steps (i.e., clustering and evaluation). The reason is because the k-means algorithm is an NP-hard problem. Under standard configuration, the algorithm will converge to a good local optimum in a reasonable time, but if the objective function changes, there is no guarantee that it will reach an acceptable optimum result.

While several modified algorithms, such as k-means++ and k-medoids, have been introduced to improve the conventional k-means, similar concerns still arise.

When the objective function in an optimization problem such as a clustering algorithm becomes more complex, the search space will become more rugged. The search algorithm may therefore not converge as expected.

Silhouette Vs. Elbow Methods.

The silhouette and elbow methods are two simple yet imperative methods that you can use to find the optimum number of clusters. The silhouette method uses the silhouette coefficient, and the elbow method uses inertia, the original scoring function in the k-means algorithm.

The latter uses a heuristic to determine the elbow of a curve as a special point. In cluster analysis, the special point indicates the optimum number of clusters. According to the literature, the elbow method is often used with inertia. Hence, the elbow method with diverse scoring functions rather than inertia is correct, although uncommon.

To evaluate a clustering method, you should utilize the silhouette technique since it uses inter-cluster and intra-cluster distances in its scoring function, contrary to the elbow method, which only uses intra-cluster distances. This does not mean, though, that the silhouette method is superior. Aside from these two approaches, many other ways exist to determine the optimum number of clusters in a dataset. I encourage you to study procedures such as the Akaike and Bayesian information criteria to learn more about this subject. These statistical measures are used for model selection, particularly in probabilistic clustering models like Gaussian Mixture Models. They balance model fit with model complexity by introducing a penalty for the number of parameters, helping to avoid overfitting. No method is particularly better than another one as they all capture various data characteristics.

The elbow method uses intra-cluster distances, while the silhouette method uses a combination of inter-cluster and intra-cluster distances. You should thus expect different results.

CHAPTER 15

How to Improve Single LLM Performance with Multi-Agent Systems

W e borrow concepts and tools from various fields to create innovative solutions for others. Years back, I used NLP concepts and tools to build a low-computation gesture recognition engine running on a microcontroller. The approach was very successful, resulting in several US patents and a successful wearable product shipped to 100K+ customers worldwide. To me, using multi-agent systems (MAS) in the context of LLMs is another example of this idea.

The AI community borrowed and mixed this concept with LLMs to address more complex tasks or questions. MAS has been a well-known field of research in AI for a long time. We have used this concept in many fields, including swarm robotics and biological-inspired optimization techniques. It is important for all of us to understand why the combination of MAS and LLMs outperforms a single LLM. If so, we can take the next step and push the performance further.

A multi-agent system is a combination of elements, or agents, that interact. Each agent has its own goals and tools. They can use many tools, such as parsers, collectors, or calculators. These agents interact in a linear sequence or a more complex structure (such as an interconnected network). We use the multi-agent system architecture for many reasons. It can solve problems that are impossible for a single agent. It has a modular and transparent architecture that leads to more efficient solutions.

Several methodologies were previously introduced to enhance the performance of a single LLM, such as chain-of-thought, self-consistency, self-reflection, and guardrailing. Using multi-AI agents is another effective approach to improving the final outcomes we want to investigate in this chapter. Here, I want to highlight the concepts we use in multi-agent systems that led to great results: (1) distributed intelligence, (2) structured prompt, and (3) enhanced context. As I said above, by leveraging ideas from the literature, we can continue improving the outcome of multi-AI agent systems.

Distributed Intelligence

For a long time, engineers have focused on designing complex mathematical models (mostly with differential equations) to describe physical, biological, and economic systems. However, they eventually discovered that designing a single model is not enough effective and accurate. They concluded that a network of simple models interacting with each other often outperforms a single complex model. This is what exactly happens in the realm of LLM. A single gigantic LLM with 100B+ parameters also suffers from issues that can not be addressed in a single model schema.

Swarm intelligence is a good example of how a network of simple models interacting with each other works effectively. For example, the ant colony optimization technique is developed based on ants' behavior of using pheromone trails to find efficient paths. In this example, ants are agents, and the pheromone trails are the communication schema. The collective outcome of ant colony behaviors, built upon simple agent tasks and extensive interactions, is far beyond the capability of a single agent. This is what exactly we have seen in the multi-AI agent systems.

In a multi-AI agent system, we have a network of agents, each powered by an LLM and a set of tools. Each agent is tuned for a specific task, such as information retrieval or summarization. The agents communicate with each other by passing data. The modular architecture of the network allows you to improve agents individually. You can collaborate with other teams to solve advanced problems, as the design of one agent doesn't interfere with the others. For example, why must you build your own summarizer agent if a high-performance agent exists?

 A single gigantic LLM with 100B+ parameters also suffers from issues that can not be addressed in a single-model schema. The solution is to use a distributed intelligence concept with a multi-model schema, which can be realized in multi-agent systems.

Structured Prompt

This may be obvious, but it is worth mentioning. The AI industry has long benefited from structured data. Many current conventional AI models work better with structured data. Why not LLMs, then?

A single complex prompt, including context and instruction, can confuse humans and LLMs. To increase clarity in complex prompts, we often use templates with a standard structure that literature has shown to be effective. This idea led the AI community to develop tools such as Outlines and LMQL, libraries to write robust and modular prompts.

Using structured prompts improves LLM results by enhancing clarity and focus. Although a structured prompt requires more initial effort, it significantly boosts the model outcome's quality, consistency, and efficiency. In multi-AI agent systems (such as the implementation made by crewAI), we use structured interfaces or prompts to define Tool, Task, and Agent (three bases of a MAS). For instance, we define role, goal, and context (called backstory in crewAI) clearly and explicitly for each Agent.

 **Vision** A single complex prompt, including context and instruction, can confuse humans and LLMs. To improve clarity and focus, we must break down complex prompts into structured, simple ones like what we have in MAS implementations.

You can find a sample of creating an agent in crewAI with the structured prompts below.

```
custom_agent = Agent(
  role = "Text",
  goal = "Text",
  backstory = "Text",
  allow_delegation = Boolean,
  verbose = Boolean
)
```

Enhanced Context

One common challenge with LLMs is that they are trained on historical data, limiting their access to the most updated information. The AI community proposed the Retrieval-Augmented Generation (RAG) technique to extract the most relevant and factual data to enhance the context of LLMs. The relevant and factual context within the prompt helps us improve the performance of the question-answer use case. A small LLM (such as Llama 8B) enhanced with RAG may work better than a huge LLM (Llama 405B) without RAG.

RAG, by itself, is a powerful technique to improve the performance of a single LLM. Within RAG, we leveraged advanced techniques such as text embedding, reranking, and format-aware chunking to extract the most relevant context for a given query. We use RAG agents in multi-AI agent systems as well. But is there any other way to enhance the context of LLMs?

RAG is not the only solution to enhance the context of LLMs. In multi-AI agent systems, we have a concept of memory, which keeps track of data generated in each step and every run to be used later in the process.

The answer is yes. In multi-AI agent systems, we can go beyond using RAG agents to enhance context. Since agents within the multi-AI agent system communicate, the data passing through must be stored in memory and used if needed. This memory enables agents to share knowledge during execution. It also helps to keep the data from previous runs and use them in the latest one. Below is a sample of creating a MAS with memory using the crewAI.

```
MAS = Crew(
  agents = [agent_1, agent_2, agent_3],
  tasks = [task_1, task_2, task_3],
  verbose = 2,
  memory = True
)
```

In multi-AI agent systems, there are three types of memory: short-term, long-term, and entity. The explanation of these types of memory is beyond the scope of this chapter.

The Last Words.

We have several methods to improve the performance of LLMs, such as chain-of-thought, self-consistency, self-reflection, and guardrailing. Another effective approach is employing multi-agent systems to enhance LLM performance in production. A multi-agent system is another methodology to improve the performance of a single LLM. A multi-AI agent system outperforms a single AI agent mainly due to the distributed intelligence, structured prompt, and enhanced context.

CHAPTER 16

The Black Swan of the AI Industry: Ensemble Classifiers

This chapter describes the significance of ensemble classifiers in the AI industry. I avoid explaining classical methods since so many other resources are readily available. What I do want to do, though, is show you the strength of ensemble classifiers (or methods) and how you can make use of them in your projects. To accomplish this, I will share the story of the ensemble classifier that my team and I invented several years back while working on the gesture control armband. Although I am naturally humble, I take a little pleasure in knowing that our ensemble classifier is still alive and kicking today, albeit under Meta (formerly named Facebook) ownership. You will find that an ensemble method, either a classic one or one that you have designed yourself, will often work much better than how you may initially have expected it to.

You will face many unknowns working in the AI industry, but regardless of the challenges, results must be delivered promptly and regularly. You usually cannot respond to these unknowns by applying time-consuming methods to train and tune classifiers. It is also important to always ensure that the classifiers you design can be enhanced in stages. The ensemble method is frequently the most correct approach to take.

First, let me tell you how the ensemble classifier we developed started. Our gesture control armband was designed to identify hand gestures based on muscle signals. It was composed of eight sensors that sat on a person's forearm and recorded muscle signals.

We were in the primary phase, and the final product was not yet ready. We wanted to develop a classifier using data collected by the prototypes. Sadly, though, we were often disappointed by the functionality of the prototypes in data recording. Sometimes, sensor data was not recorded due to firmware issues; at other times, the sensors captured altered signals due to changes made by our electrical engineering team. In short, whatever the reason, the quality of the training data was not reliable at any level during the preliminary stages of development.

We were also not sure about what gestures to target. We had identified five hand gestures (Left, Right, Fist, Spread, and Snap), but we did not know for certain if these were the five best gestures to target from the customer's point of view or if there were other ones that we had not considered. In other words, business requirements had not yet been determined. Nevertheless, in the project's early days, and without sufficient demonstrations and tests having been conducted, we were still required to design a workable gesture recognition engine.

A Base Classifier Does Not Need To Be A Weak Classifier.

It is always recommended to build a model based on a large volume of data. For us, the quality of data recorded by our prototypes was poor, and the use cases were not yet solidified. Given that, our efforts to collect a large volume of data with our prototypes might very well have turned out to be a waste of time. (As an aside, Chapter 8 details some of the significant issues that can arise when conducting large-scale data collection.)

Hence, I designed a base classifier that did not require as much data. The base classifier was a vector classifier that used cosine similarity, a standard similarity metric, to evaluate the class membership. As expected, its performance was mediocre at best, but much better than a weak classifier (in general terms, you will find that a weak classifier usually works slightly better than a random classifier). I then used the vector classifier as the base classifier for our future development.

These were our first, and perhaps not so promising, steps to design an ensemble method that in the end was successful and continues today under Facebook ownership.

 When the data collection setup is not yet ready, you should design base classifiers that do not necessitate as much data.

The Base Classifiers Should Be Built Upon The Same Algorithm.

The purpose of an ensemble classifier is to aggregate several different classifiers regardless of their type or algorithm. I therefore recommend that the base classifiers you design all have a similar algorithm. If you are wondering why I made that recommendation, please read on.

For this specific project, I developed a large number of simple base classifiers with a similar algorithm rather than a few base classifiers with different algorithms. This intuitive decision was inspired by my study of the Random Forest method, where base classifiers share a similar algorithm. Another ensemble method you may likely be familiar with is AdaBoost. Its algorithm aggregates a series of one-level decision trees (also known as stump) in order to enhance the final result.

Having similar base classifiers also allowed me to gain better insight into the ensemble classifier and, thus, more control over its evolution. In other words, I could modify the base classifiers when needed since their behavior had been extensively studied during the design process. The next question for our team was to identify how best to aggregate the base classifiers.

> **Tip**
>
> Use the same algorithm for all of the base classifiers you develop. This will provide you with a better chance of having control over the evolution of your ensemble classifier.

The Strategy To Aggregate Base Classifiers Must Be Well-Designed.

Below are three classic strategies for aggregating base classifiers. I explain which strategy we utilized after this overview.

- Strategy I (Attention Mechanism)
  The algorithm adaptively learns the base classifiers using exaggeration or attention mechanisms in a sequence schema. This means the algorithm pays more attention to the data where the base classifiers failed in each step, reducing the prediction bias. In other words, the next classifier in the sequence is trained to address the misclassified data from the previous step. These methods are often called Boosting. Figure 5 below is a visual representation of this strategy.

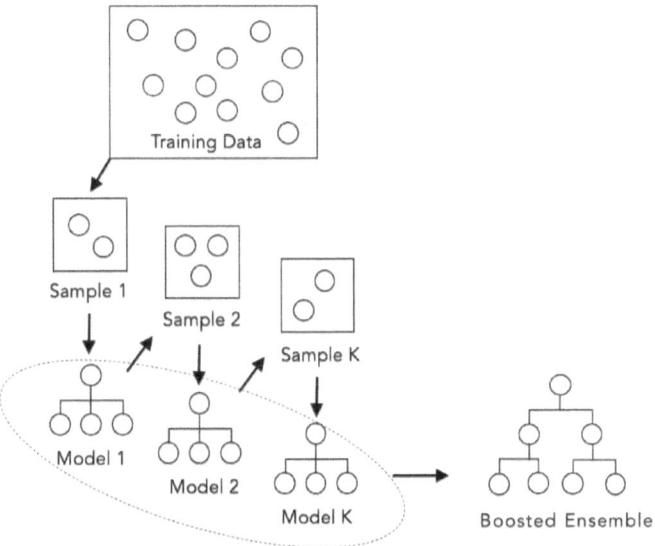

Figure 5- Strategy I: Attention Mechanism.

- ■ Strategy II (Data Split)

  The algorithm learns the base classifiers in parallel with no interaction. Each base classifier is learned on a randomly generated set of data that exists in the training dataset, reducing the variance in the prediction. These methods are often called Bagging. Figure 6 below is a visual representation of this strategy.

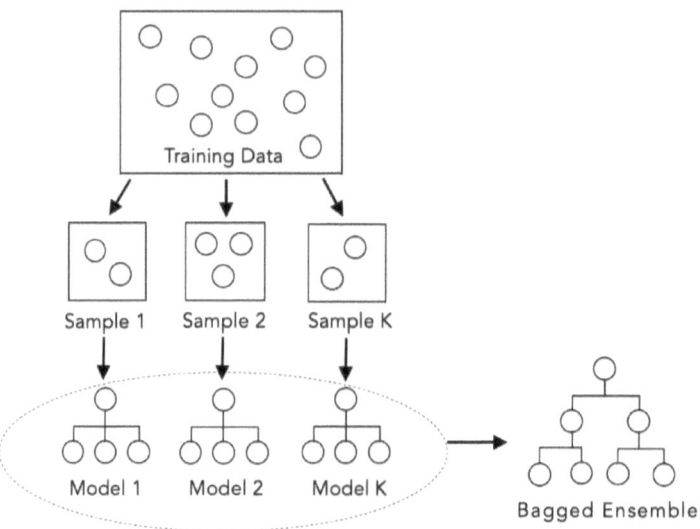

Figure 6- Strategy II: Data Split.

■ Strategy III (Model Stacking)

The algorithm learns the base classifiers in parallel with no interaction. Each base classifier is learned on the entire training dataset. The algorithm then combines the results of the base classifiers by training a meta-model that takes the preliminary results and creates the final prediction. Figure 7 below is a visual representation of this strategy. (Do note that the meta-model designed for this strategy need not be complex. It can simply be, for example, a straightforward voting classifier.)

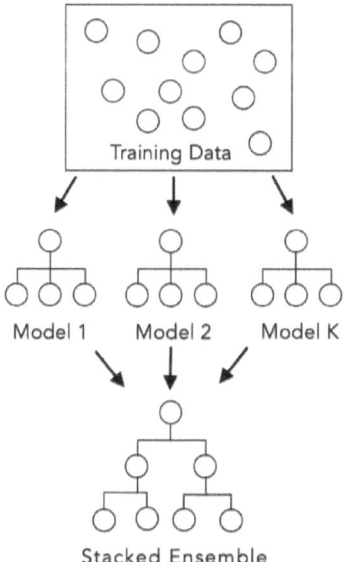

Figure 7- Strategy III: Model Stacking.

With that background information out of the way, I now want to describe how we went about selecting a strategy to aggregate the results of base classifiers.

Our team's goal was to have the gadget work without flaws for a large group rather than just work satisfactorily for everyone. This is a classic example of the bias-variance tradeoff that always exists in machine learning problems. We decided to tackle this challenge with a creative approach that would not be found within the textbook suggestions.

We therefore introduced two models: (a) the population model and (b) the personalized model. The population model was targeted to work for a large group but not for everyone. This model was learned using the training dataset. The personalized model was targeted to work for a small group of those who experienced only mediocre/average results when using the population model. This model was trained using a person's data recorded in each session of use.

In short, we decided to improve bias with less attention to variance in the population model. Thus, Strategy II, which aims to reduce variance, could not be a choice.

We also had another challenge to overcome. Users could wear the gadget in numerous ways, and those different ways result in different input data. Hence, the base classifiers had to be adjusted each time a user wore the gadget. We spent much time and energy developing an algorithm that could efficiently adjust the base classifiers. In boosting algorithms, base classifiers are designed in a sequence schema that creates interdependencies and complexities. Therefore, Strategy I could not be a choice either.

Tip

To build a strong classifier, you should aggregate many simple base classifiers using a model stacking approach. Although you should train your base classifiers with the same algorithm, you can make use of different datasets and/or hyperparameter tuning in the training process.

As you may have guessed by now, we selected Strategy III, the model stacking strategy. The meta-model that we designed was a combination of a probabilistic classifier and a voting mechanism. Since we worked with time-series data of an unfixed length (for example, a gesture might take one second, and another gesture could take two seconds), a considerable amount of hyperparameter tuning was incorporated into the training process. The model stacking strategy, with a large number of flexible base classifiers, solved our problem.

The Last Words.

In industry, while many unknowns will ensue, you will find that results are nevertheless demanded often. Those results will not materialize when time-consuming methods are applied to train and tune classifiers. Since you want to ensure that the classifiers you design can be enhanced in the future, the ensemble method is a very suitable approach.

Although it would be ideal to be able to develop a generalized technique that can address diverse problems, the reality is that you may never be able to invent such a method. Based on my own experiences, I know you will rarely regret targeting an industry problem with an ensemble approach. And why do I say that? In short, the philosophy behind ensemble methods is to use the "wisdom of weighted crowds of experts."

I must add, as an aside, that I love this expression! It is a quote from an artificial intelligence course taught by the late Professor Patrick Winston in MIT OpenCourseWare. You will read later on, in Chapter 19, that I recommend his courses for personal study.

CHAPTER 17

The Key to Success: Experiment Management Systems

To build an AI product, numerous models with different parameter configurations must be trained using a training dataset that evolves. In addition, the metrics evaluating model performance should also be altered according to the situation. As an AI engineer, you must manage this complicated process and be ready on short notice to deploy the best model suitable for each scenario. A technology that manages this process is thus essential.

Experiment Management Systems Vs. Version Control Systems.

In software development, version control systems (or VCS) such as Git technology and various workflow structures allow you to track code changes and manage software versions. This technology expedites the development process and enables collaboration. Unfortunately, due primarily to its complexity, there is still no single well-adapted management system in machine learning.

In the machine learning context, the term "experiment" is often used instead of the term "version." An experiment has a much broader definition compared to a version. An experiment is a series of research and development tasks to train a model. The experiment may fail or succeed, but regardless, it is tagged with various artifacts such as ML models, performance reports, and log files. The experiment management system (or EMS) is the version control system in the AI context. In this chapter, you will find answers to questions such as

"Why is an experiment management system needed?" and "What are the criteria for a useful EMS?"

Why Do You Need To Use An Experiment Management System?

From The Perspective Of The Development Team.

An experiment may fail or succeed, while a version is focused on tracking the past. This is the first difference between software development and machine learning development. In the former, a VCS enables you to track the development path; in the latter, an EMS allows you to find the path to success. An AI team must conduct many experiments to build an ML model that meets the acceptance criteria. These experiments must be recorded and archived for further analysis to be shared within the team. An EMS benefits the engineers working on a project and helps the product or technical managers track the development progress.

| | The two keys to success in building an AI product are (1) to systematically conduct experiments with different hypotheses and (2) to always be learning from the past in order to be continually enhancing your understanding of the problem you are presently facing. |

From The Perspective Of The Product Team.

An experiment is associated with artifacts such as the ML model and metadata such as performance metrics. This helps restore past models according to the product team's requests. For example, it sometimes happens that the deployed model (also known as the production model) does not function as needed. In this case, the development team must retrieve and deploy one of the past functional models, as there is no time to run new experiments in an emergency.

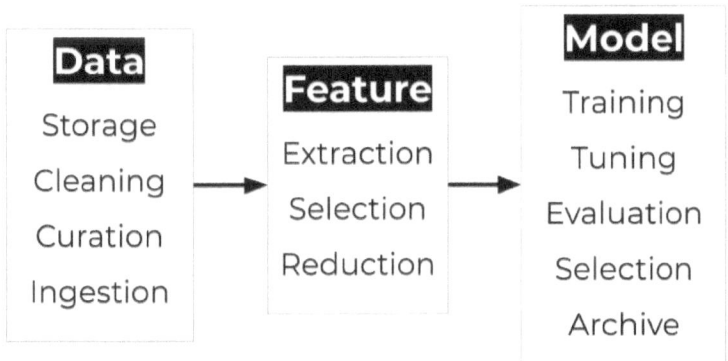

Figure 8- The high-level development pipeline in machine learning. A helpful EMS must track changes in the whole pipeline.

What Are The Criteria For A Good Experiment Management System?

A basic EMS in artificial intelligence must archive models and performance metrics. It also must let users search among models. As you can deduce, the basic functionalities refer to model training.

An advanced EMS must track changes in the entire pipeline and even automate the trials (for example, the model training and hyperparameter tuning processes). Do remember that any experiment you conduct must be reproducible. Reproducibility is one of the principles of science. If an EMS solution does not track changes in the complete pipeline, it seldom allows you to reproduce the experiment. Figure 8 above is an image of the high-level development pipeline in machine learning.

In recent years, several EMS solutions have been developed, such as "MLflow," "Neptune," and "Guild." Since there is no perfect universal solution on the market, you need to determine what your project will entail and then select the EMS solution based on that. For instance, Neptune may serve you better if your daily tasks include considerable research and you need to collaborate within a team. On the other hand, if you will primarily require an EMS to automate hyperparameter tuning, you should use Guild.

The Last Words.

These days, most of the EMS solutions work as a wrapper on top of your code. That is why you need to add several lines of code to your scripts before starting to use the service. Most importantly, an EMS should be used to resolve development issues. However, an EMS solution can also be a source of confusion rather than productivity, similar to version control systems in software development.

In artificial intelligence, just like in other fields of science, it is best to adopt the science workflow. A science workflow includes the following steps:

- drive a hypothesis to build a solution,
- conduct a reproducible experiment to test the hypothesis,
- analyze your results and learn from the past,
- drive a new hypothesis that brings you a step closer to your objectives and
- conduct this process again and again until you have satisfied your main requirements.

In short, an EMS solution is an essential tool for implementing the data science workflow and building a successful AI product.

CHAPTER 18

The Key to Success: Explainable AI

The Explainable AI (XAI) tools are crucial in building trust among end-users and regulators, identifying and mitigating bias, and improving overall model performance. They are built to answer the main question of all users: "Why did the model make a specific prediction for an instance or a group of instances?" The AI community has introduced various concepts and tools to interpret AI model outcomes, including feature importance, partial dependence plots, and sub-population analysis.

While the XAI tools are invaluable in identifying bias and building trust, they are highly susceptible to misuse. For instance, most feature importance methods assume that features are independent. As a result, including highly correlated features in the analysis can lead to unreliable outcomes. Moreover, different approaches for calculating the global importance of features, such as using the "mean absolute value" or the "max absolute value," can lead to inconsistent results.

Before reading this chapter, you should be familiar with feature importance, partial dependence plot, and sub-population analysis; otherwise, you may not benefit adequately. If you are already familiar with these concepts, this chapter will introduce you to new scenarios you may not have encountered. These lessons are based on my experience delivering solutions to enterprise clients in the past few years.

Feature Importance

Feature importance refers to a family of techniques used to determine the significance of individual features in contributing to the predictions made by a machine learning model. Imagine you are trying to predict something, like the price of a house, using features like the number of bedrooms, location, and size. Feature importance tells you which of these factors has the most impact on the house price. There are two different categories of feature importance tools: model-specific and model-agnostic.

Model-specific tools are limited to specific model types, such as coefficient-based and tree-based models. For instance, the magnitude of the coefficients in linear models can be used as an indicator of feature importance. Larger coefficients suggest greater importance. The Gini impurity is a specific measure in the tree-based models that shows the importance of a feature.

Model-agnostic tools include many techniques, such as Shapley values, LIME, and Permutation Feature Importance (PFI). Shapley values and LIME are local methods suitable for explaining individual predictions, while PFI is a global method used to assess the importance of features across the entire population. Here, I focus on the PFI technique and its limitations as a method for ranking the importance of all features in the entire dataset.

The PFI technique involves shuffling the values of each feature and observing how the model's performance (e.g., accuracy or RMSE) changes using a global measure (e.g., mean absolute value or max absolute value). If shuffling a feature significantly degrades the model's performance, that feature is deemed important. Shuffling can be done in different ways, such as replacing feature values with those randomly selected from the overall data distribution or using values that reflect the local structure of the data.

Notes to consider.

- Various factors (such as the model type, model convergence, and the choice of global measure) impact the feature importance results. Therefore, before using the final results, ensure the outcome is repeatable and consistent with different models and runs. If the final results get changed with different models, how would you want to rely on them?

- Make sure there are no correlated features in the list of features. The algorithm is designed with the assumption that features are independent, and if the highly correlated features exist in the data, the results are not reliable.

- You must note that the global measure is sensitive to the scale and variance of the data. If you use "max absolute value" as your global measure within non-normalized data, a feature with a larger scale will most likely end up on the first rank of your feature importance list. So, make sure to normalize data or choose the global measure wisely.

Partial Dependence Plot

The partial dependence plot (PDP) shows the marginal effect of one feature on the predicted outcome of a machine learning model. It shows whether the relationship between the target and a feature is linear, monotonic, or more complex. For instance, if you run the PDP analysis on a linear regression model, it will show a linear relationship across all features.

Notes to consider.

- A flat partial dependence plot suggests that the feature is unimportant, while more variation suggests a greater influence. If you encounter a feature with a flat PDP, consider removing it from your model. However, you must always validate the impact of feature removal by checking model performance, as PDPs present the marginal effect, and a flat PDP may not reflect the feature's importance across the entire feature space.

Tip

A flat partial dependence plot suggests that the feature is unimportant, while more variation suggests a greater influence.

- If the partial dependence plot shows a value of 1 for a specific category in a categorical variable, it suggests that this category highly influences the model's predicted outcome. This requires further investigation, as it may indicate data imbalance, overfitting, or data leakage.
- For example, in a customer churn analysis, if you use a feature like is_deceased, a value of "Yes" indicates that the customer is deceased and has consequently churned. However, if the value is "No," it provides no additional information. This is an example of a "data leakage" issue. On another note, if you are dealing with an overfitting issue, you can consider creating new categorical variables with another binning strategy to mitigate the dominance of one category and train a more generalizable model.

Subpopulation Analysis

The subpopulation analysis assesses whether the model performs consistently across different groups (subpopulations). If the model predicts outcomes significantly better for one group than another, it may indicate bias. While achieving identical performance across all groups is unrealistic, substantial differences mean bias. There are two methods to identify bias.

First, you must split the data into subgroups based on specific characteristics (e.g., age or gender) and evaluate the model's performance separately for each group. Analyzing the model's performances across all groups allows you to identify bias in the model.

Second, you must review the PDP results, particularly for categorical features. If the PDP values vary significantly within a categorical variable, it indicates that the model is particularly sensitive to a specific category. This sensitivity may cause the model's outcomes to be biased toward the category with the highest value.

Notes to consider.

- Identifying bias is often straightforward, but addressing it can be challenging. Bias frequently stems from imbalanced data. Stratified K-Fold cross-validation is an effective technique for managing such datasets. When your data has uneven class distribution (e.g., one class is significantly more prevalent), Stratified K-Fold ensures that each fold maintains the same class proportions as the original dataset. This approach helps in developing less biased models.

■ If stratified cross-validation does not eliminate the bias, you may need to develop separate models for each group, particularly if the data behaves differently across those groups. This approach allows each model to be tailored to the unique characteristics of each subgroup, potentially improving overall performance. Dividing the data into meaningful groups can also enhance the explainability of the models.

Part 4: Learn More

CHAPTER 19

The Best Online Artificial Intelligence Courses

A lthough you can easily find numerous artificial intelligence courses online, you may be uncertain whether the one(s) you have chosen will serve you well. For instance, you may want to learn the pure math behind machine learning algorithms to enhance your knowledge. On the other hand, you may be preparing for a job interview and require a refresher course on some aspect of AI.

In this chapter, I have gathered together in one place information on several free machine learning courses. Each of these courses can be considered, at least in some respect, unique. Since I have taken these courses in part or full, I can honestly and without hesitation recommend them to you. This chapter explains why these courses are distinctive and who might be able to take the best advantage of them. These courses are well-suited for a variety of learning styles and educational purposes. I know they will save you time and energy in your journey to learn machine learning and artificial intelligence. I hope you find them helpful.

Explaining Math Without Oversimplifying It.

If you love pure math, I recommend a YouTube channel called "mathematicalmonk." Although the instructor's identity is unknown, the channel has over 80K happy subscribers at the time of writing. They teach some of the most reliable classic machine learning courses out there. Nothing can beat this program if you want to learn the math behind algorithms. I took these courses years ago and still refer back to the channel whenever necessary.

Gain Insight Into Various AI Methods.

To become an expert on a topic, you must gain insight. It is admirable to have a surface-level understanding of algorithms and methodologies, for example, but you cannot solve critical problems without knowing the underlying facts. To do just that, I encourage you to check out the Artificial Intelligence course (course number: 6-034F10) of the MIT OpenCourseWare project on YouTube.

Since these are AI courses, they cover topics beyond machine learning. The instructor, the late Professor Patrick Winston, was a world-renowned lecturer, and he will grab your attention in seconds. I know you will continue watching all the videos after viewing the first one. These courses are available on the YouTube channel of the MIT OCW project. OpenCourseWare (OCW) is an extraordinary venture launched by the Massachusetts Institute of Technology (MIT) in 2002.

A Great Combination Of Math And Visuals.

A picture is definitely worth (at least) a thousand words. StatQuest is a YouTube channel with about 466K subscribers at the time of writing. It provides a perfect combination of math and visuals. The lectures are laser-focused and as brief as possible. In addition, the instructor, Joshua Starmer, teaches the courses in such a manner that it would be impossible for you to find yourself bored. His courses are well worth exploring if, for instance, you need to prepare for a job interview but are pressed for time. Once, I wanted to know more about a relatively new boosting algorithm called XGBoost, and this channel helped me quickly learn everything I needed to know.

The Best Introductory Deep Learning Course.

The MIT course, "Introduction to Deep Learning," is a fantastic collection of the latest deep learning materials. If you are looking for a deep learning course that takes a practical approach and combines fundamental knowledge with coding experience and cool applications, I highly recommend it. They maintain the ideal balance of everything you could possibly want in an educational video. This is an introductory course, so do not expect in-depth lessons on computer vision or natural language processing. However, it will shed light on your path to learning about the latest advancements in this field.

Essential Development Tools By Google.

AI Adventures is an excellent series of videos covering AI development topics. It is available on the Google Cloud Tech YouTube channel. If you already know machine learning concepts, this is the consummate vehicle to learn crucial development tools. You will not become an expert in developing machine learning solutions by taking an online course or two, but these videos provide a very decent introduction to essential development tools.

Unorthodox Lessons From The Python Community.

Python is the mainstream programming language for AI development. You can find a multitude of open-source projects online that will expedite your growth in Python. A Python community named PyData runs many events around the world, and they share videos of these occasions on a YouTube channel named after the community. The PyData channel has more than 114K subscribers at the time of writing. Their videos cover a gamut of topics, including coding, and they provide a plethora of practical tips related to Python.